The President and Congress

**FOUNDATIONS OF AMERICAN GOVERNMENT
AND POLITICAL SCIENCE**

Joseph P. Harris, Consulting Editor

The purpose of this series is to provide a group of relatively short treatises on major aspects of government in modern society. Each volume introduces the reader to a major field of political science through a discussion of important issues, problems, processes, and forces and at the same time includes an account of American political institutions. Each is the work of a distinguished scholar who is a specialist in and teaches the subjects covered. Together the volumes can well serve the needs of introductory courses in American government and political science.

ANDREW HACKER: The Study of Politics: The Western Tradition and American Origins

C. HERMAN PRITCHETT: The American Constitutional System

HUGH A. BONE and AUSTIN RANNEY: Politics and Voters

ROWLAND EGGER and JOSEPH P. HARRIS: The President and Congress

JOHN J. CORSON and JOSEPH P. HARRIS: Public Administration in Modern Society

CHARLES O. LERCHE, JR.: America in World Affairs

CHARLES R. ADRIAN: Governing Our Fifty States and Their Communities

THE PRESIDENT
AND CONGRESS

Rowland Egger

Professor of Political Science and
Edward R. Stettinius Professor of Foreign Affairs
University of Virginia

Joseph P. Harris

Professor of Political Science
University of California, Berkeley

McGRAW-HILL BOOK COMPANY, INC.
NEW YORK / SAN FRANCISCO /
TORONTO / LONDON

*This book is set in linotype Janson. The
original specimen sheets date from about
1700 and are of Dutch origin. The chapter
openings are Century Bold Condensed and
the displayed heads are News Gothic Bold.*

Preface

This volume on the President and Congress examines the ways in which these two political and governmental institutions have developed and the ways in which they manage their relationships with each other. One of the fundamental theories upon which the American government is based is the liberty of the individual. One of the basic principles which is incorporated in the Constitution for the purpose of preserving individual liberty is the separation of powers and the system of checks and balances. Although the President and Congress are, within their respective spheres, independent and coequal, for almost all important purposes they must reach some sort of agreement before either can perform the duties for which it is responsible under the Constitution. They are therefore necessarily involved in a constant struggle to persuade and influence each other on vital public issues. This struggle reaches into the halls of Congress, and the committees and subcommittees of the houses on the one hand, and into the departments, bureaus, and agencies of the executive branch on the other.

The book has a certain bias, which may well be admitted at the outset. The authors are, in general, convinced that the President, representing the whole nation, is more successful in discerning the national interest and defining the national purpose than is the Congress, the members of which represent only parts of the whole and are, by definition, likely to inform their actions in accordance with the limited constituencies and special interests which determine their election. Other writers entertain contrary views. The student must arrive at his own conclusions. The important thing is that he understand the reasons for the conclusions which he may eventually reach.

Rowland Egger
Joseph P. Harris

Contents

1 THE PRESIDENCY: HISTORY AND POWERS, 1

The Nature of the Presidential Office
The Expansion of Presidential Power
The Right to Be Consulted
The Right to Encourage
The Right to Warn

2 PRESIDENTIAL LEADERSHIP, 21

The President as Chief Executive
The President as Chief Administrator
The President and Foreign Policy
The President as Commander in Chief
The President and Internal Security

3 THE PRESIDENT AND CONGRESS, 42

Presidentialism and Congressionalism
The Imperatives of Presidential Leadership
Constitutional Powers of Leadership
Political Powers of Leadership
Perespectives of Cooperation

4 CONGRESS: FUNCTIONS AND ORGANIZATION, 61

Functions and Powers
The Adoption of a Bicameral Legislature
The House of Representatives
The Senate
The Committee System

5 THE LEGISLATIVE PROCESS, 82

The Origin of Bills
The Legislative Struggle
Procedure in the House
Procedure in the Senate

6 CONGRESS: THE GRAND INQUEST OF THE NATION, 101

The Conduct of Investigations
Congressional Control of Administration
The Reorganization and Reform of Congress

FOR FURTHER READING, 119

INDEX, 123

The President and Congress

THE PRESIDENCY: HISTORY AND POWERS

Chapter 1

THE NATURE OF THE PRESIDENTIAL OFFICE

The American Presidency is one of the profound paradoxes of history. It is the most majestic democratic executive office of modern times. But its majesty rests upon a singularly modest grant of constitutional authority, as well as a pervading suspicion of executive power. It was designed to be aloof from the clamor of the crowd. But it has developed a relationship of intimacy with the mainstream of public opinion unique in the annals of politics. The government of which the Presidency is the symbolic manifestation is the instrument of a great welfare state. But its constitutional foundations were erected upon a deep distrust of central government, and a reluctant acceptance of even the minimum conditions of national unity. The President of the United States bears almost the entire burden of the formulation of national policy and the definition of the national purpose. But it is generally supposed, and the Constitution seems to have intended, that he is formally responsible for little more than the faithful execution of the laws which are enacted by Congress and interpreted by the Supreme Court.

Many books have been written about the American Presidency, and some of the finest literature in the field of political science has been concerned with it. The presidential office has been described by many different men as many different things. To some the Presidency is a problem in constitutional law. To others the President has appeared primarily as a party leader. Some writers have been intrigued with the President's role as Commander in Chief. Still others have viewed the Presidency from the vantage point of administrative leadership of the Federal bureaucracy. The tasks of the President in respect to the national welfare and security have preempted the attention of many writers, and his responsibilities in the field of foreign affairs have been the focus of much analysis and speculation. The role of the President in the leadership of Congress and in the preparation and enactment of legislation is also the subject of considerable literature. More recently, the ways in which Presidents create and consolidate situations of power have fallen under scientific scrutiny. The autobiographies of the Presidents themselves not unnaturally stress the President's role as moral leader.

An understanding of the Presidency involves the appreciation of all these facets of the presidential office. But it involves something in addition. The Presidency is much more than the sum of its parts—of the mere aggregation of its power and functions. Every man who has ever served as President of the United States has added something to—and perhaps subtracted something from—the role of the Presidency during his incumbency. He has been, in the dichotomy of Theodore Roosevelt, a "Lincoln" President or a "Buchanan" President, or more likely he has from time to time been both. But he has not basically altered the essential character of the office or affected its potential. The President today is involved in many more activities than, and in activities quite different from, those which demanded the attention of George

Washington. But the place of the President at the apex of national political life has not been altered. Indeed, because the Presidency is in a much more fundamental sense a creation of the American culture and the American tradition than it is of the Constitution or the statutes, the machinery of government or the administrative process, it can be adequately understood only within this wider social context.

Students of the Presidency have not been unaware of this fact. They have repeatedly observed that the American system of government has in effect revived the elective kingship. But they have treated the observation merely as an epigram, whereas it is in fact a definition. The proximate genus to the Presidency is kingship. The essential difference is that the office is elective. Both elements of the definition are indispensable. If the President were not a king, the system could not survive. If he were not elective, he could not be trusted with the powers he must exercise if the system is to survive.

THE EXPANSION OF PRESIDENTIAL POWER

In an era in which many monarchies have disappeared, and the power of kings all over the world has declined, the power of the President has enormously increased. Moreover, the power of the President has not been expanded by reason of constitutional amendment, or of any fundamental alteration in the legal aspects of the balance of power among the three branches of the government. It has increased through subtle and usually informal changes, attributable mainly to the fact that the President is the literal incarnation of American mass democracy.

It was not planned that way. The procedure established in the Constitution for the selection of the President was calculated to secure a quite different result. The electoral college provided for in Article II was contemplated to operate as a sort of super civil service commission, and to select from among all eligible Americans of stature sufficient to recommend themselves to the electors the two "best" men. The one receiving the highest number of electoral votes was to be the President, and the one receiving the next-highest number was to be Vice President. But the purport of the process was to remove the election of the President from direct contact with politics, and to return the control of the government to an aloof, if "enlightened" gentry.

History plays many a trick on constitution makers. The rise of the party system within a few years after the adoption of the Constitution, and the Twelfth Amendment adopted in 1804 providing for separate voting for President and Vice President converted the electoral college into an instrument for the merely formal ratification of a decision taken many weeks earlier at the polls. The abolition of congressional caucuses for the selection of candidates substantially deemphasized the role of legislative party leaders in the nominating process. And the election of Andrew Jackson in 1829 marked the irrevocable union between the President and the people which has been the bellwether of presidential power and prestige ever since. The Presidency might not be less lonely, but it would never again be aloof. And Jackson's Whiggish enemies were more right than they knew when they called him in vituperation "King Andrew."

Some other decisions of the Philadelphia Convention were likewise important in making the development of presidential hegemony possible, and in some senses inevitable. The first of these concerned the unity of the Presidency—the vesting of executive power in a single person rather than in a council. The second concerned the independence of the Presidency—the creation of an office which exercises its powers independently of any other organ of the government. From these two basic decisions many others flowed, such as the electoral machinery established by the Constitution, a fixed term for the President, presidential reeligibility, the constitutional specification of executive powers, the rejection of a council to second-guess the President on nominations and appointments, vetoes, and other acts, and the prohibition of simultaneous occupancy of executive and legislative posts. A third basic decision—to give the President a substantial part of the royal prerogative with respect to military and diplomatic affairs—laid the groundwork for a steady accretion of presidential power the full dimensions of which are not even now clearly evident. The aggregate effect of these decisions was to create an American Presidency capable of both lending impetus and responding to the rise of American democracy. The stature of the Presidency at any point in time is directly proportional to the forward thrust of democratic forces in the national life. This forward thrust—erratically and discontinuously, to be sure— has been in the ascendant almost from the beginnings of the nation.

The explanation of the aggrandizement of the President's power lies not in any quantitative assessment of presidential versus congressional or judicial influence. Nor do the asseverations of some critics concerning presidential or congressional "usurpations" shed any real light on the problem. There has been no fixed intention to subvert the separation of powers either on the part of the Congress or the President.

But there has been a profound qualitative change in the roles of the President, the Congress, and for that matter of the Court, which the gentlemen of the Philadelphia Convention never contemplated. These qualitative changes, which have produced a governmental system characterized more significantly by the interpenetration of powers than by their separation, have in turn derived from influences largely independent of formal national constitutional or legal arrangements.

The first of these influences has been the rise of American democracy, to which reference has already been made. This was undoubtedly given impetus by the settlement of the Western states and the emergence of a culture which bore few of the stigmata of caste and inequality common along the Eastern seaboard. Their constitutions were much more democratic with respect to requirements for voting, for serving in public office, and for public participation in governmental affairs generally. But at the same time the growth of industrial centers and the rising tide of European immigration were producing equally profound changes in the East, and by 1856 property qualifications for the right to vote had disappeared. Practically all white male citizens throughout the country had the right to vote. In the same period property requirements for the holding of public office, religious qualifications, and other restrictions were largely eliminated. By 1828 the popular selection of presidential electors, rather than their election by the state legislatures, had become all but universal. This change established a direct connection between the President and the people, which constitutes the most important single bulwark of presidential influence and leadership. All these powerful democratizing forces, it should be noted, were set in motion by the states, not by the national government.

Other democratizing influences likewise destined greatly to enhance presidential leadership were at work, this time in the parties. From the end of Washington's second term until the Jackson era, candidates of the parties had been selected in caucuses of the members of each party in Congress. In 1828, however, Jackson's followers disavowed the caucus as antidemocratic and unconstitutional. In 1831 the Anti-Masonic Party and the Whigs each held conventions to nominate candidates, and by 1840 the national convention had become an established American political institution. The substitution of the national party convention, made up of party members alleged to be "fresh from the people," for the legislative caucus did not destroy the influence of congressional party leaders, but it did relegate congressional leadership to a role distinctly secondary to that of the candidate.

The second force making for the aggrandizement of presidential power has been the emergence of the "positive" state, which has been brought about mainly by industrialization, urbanization, and the development of a national, rather than a sectional or local, economy and society, and by the enormous growth in modern times of economic democracy. To meet the conditions produced by this fundamental change in our way of life, the national government—more often than not under presidential leadership—has established a large number of programs of social and economic amelioration, designed to stabilize the economy and to promote higher standards of living and of public welfare. It has created a vast administrative machinery to carry out these objectives, and while most of the programs are actually operated by state and local instrumentalities, the national government remains the primary source of funds and of political and administrative direction. Most of these operations fall within the general budgetary control of the President, and in many he exercises program and administrative supervision. His obligation to see that the laws are faithfully executed is coterminous with the applicability of the laws themselves.

The notions of the opponents of a strong Presidency in 1789 were grounded in the belief inherited from the English Whigs that legislative power was in its nature popular and executive power was in its nature monarchical, and at that point in time they equated monarchical with tyrannical. From this premise they drew the conclusion that the Presidency should, in the words of Sherman, be "nothing more than an institution for carrying the will of the Legislature into effect." Gouverneur Morris, arguing for a strong Presidency, expressed a contrary view:[1]

> It is necessary that the Executive Magistrate should be the guardian of the people, even of the lower classes, agst. Legislative tyranny, against the Great & the wealthy who in the course of things will necessarily compose—the Legislative body. Wealth tends to corrupt the mind & nourish its love of power, and to stimulate it to oppression. History proves this to be the spirit of the opulent. . . . The Executive therefore ought to be so constituted as to be the great protector of the Mass of the people. . . .

[1] Max Farrand, *The Records of the Federal Convention,* Yale University Press, New Haven, Conn., 1911; vol. I, pp. 65–97; vol. II, pp. 29–105.

The opponents of an independent Presidency lost their argument in the Constitutional Convention, and time has clearly demonstrated that their basic assumption, at least as far as the American Presidency is concerned, was in grievous error. And Gouverneur Morris, like many seers whose prophecies come true, was right for the wrong reasons. The executive power turned out to be the popular power. It has protected the masses of the people. But the significant threat to the interests of the masses has not been malefactors of great wealth in the legislative branch. It has rather been the inertia and stagnation inherent in the fundamental and organic inability of Congress to initiate and take the leadership in the formulation of public policy.

Much of this inertia is attributable to the dispersive pulls created by the local basis of Congressional representation. Members of the House and of the Senate are elected from local constituencies. They look forward to being reelected from local constituencies. The pressures upon them while they are in Congress come from local constituencies. It is small wonder, therefore, that their preoccupation should be with the interests of their constituencies first, and with the national interest second if at all. And there are other dispersive influences. Fritz Morstein Marx[2] says:

> A parallel pull allied in many ways with the local, arises from the competitive advantages which the special interest enjoys over the general. By comparison with matters of general importance, the special interest is favored by its single-mindedness as well as by its bread-and-butter persistence, and both together are usually able to support a superior organization. It is a rare feat for the representative singly to be equal to these constant pulls and thus qualify himself for consideration of the common good. . . .

In addition to the dispersive influences of the local basis of representation in the legislative branch, and its peculiar vulnerability to domination by special interests, the internal organization of Congress has further impaired its ability to initiate or lead in the formulation of public policy. Congress is not a unified body. It is not even two houses. It is a loose confederation of standing, select, and joint committees.

[2] "Party Responsibility and Legislative Program," *Columbia Law Review*, vol. 30, pp. 281–299, March, 1950.

each going its own way almost entirely without reference to other committees or, for that matter, to the House or Senate. Many of the committees are further fragmented into subcommittees, equally autonomous. It is not too much to say, in fact, that Congress has virtually abdicated its corporate functions. In the main the two chambers meet merely to offer formal ratification, without real consideration, to committee and subcommittee decisions. These are not the preconditions of congressional leadership in public policy. Such a group of men, organized and proceeding in such a way, could not speak otherwise than with a multitude of voices and an utter confusion of tongues.

Finally, the march of events has been on the side of aggrandizement of presidential power. Clinton Rossiter lays it down as an axiom of political science that "great emergencies in the life of a constitutional state bring an increase in executive power and prestige, always at least temporarily, more often than not permanently."[3] Certainly, the history of the American Presidency both at home and abroad supports this view. Jackson's vigor in meeting the threat of the South Carolina Nullificationists, Lincoln's response to the forces of secession, Wilson's decision to take the nation into World War I, Franklin D. Roosevelt's mobilization of the country to fight economic stagnation and collapse and later to prosecute World War II, Truman's commitment of American forces in Korea, and continuing presidential leadership in the containment of Communist imperialism—all have brought substantial increments to the power and prestige of the office. The outlook, moreover, is for an unremitting increase in presidential responsibility and authority as the foreign relations of the United States continue to dominate almost all aspects of the public policy process. For under the Constitution, the initiative in foreign affairs lies with the President. And in a world in crisis, the power to initiate more often than not is the power to decide.

THE RIGHT TO BE CONSULTED

About one hundred years ago Walter Bagehot,[4] writing of the English monarchy as he conceived it at that time, defined the essential conditions of the exercise of sovereign leadership in a democratic society in these words:

[3] *The American Presidency*, Harcourt, Brace & World, Inc., New York, 1960, p. 86.
[4] *The English Constitution*, World's Classics ed., Oxford University Press, London, 1940, p. 67.

> To state the matter shortly, the sovereign has, under a constitutional monarchy such as ours, three rights —the right to be consulted, the right to encourage, the right to warn. And a king of great sense and sagacity would want no others. He would find that his having no others would enable him to use these with singular effect.

It has been suggested that Bagehot's concepts, obviously 80 years out of date for England, are still probably 20 years too early for the United States. Nevertheless, these three rights, writ exceedingly large, are the important rights of the President of the United States. And the Presidents best remembered as men of great sense and sagacity have relied primarily on these rights in the exercise of their leadership.

The first of these, the right to be consulted, is a potent source of influence and authority. What does it mean? Bagehot[5] illustrates his conception of the right to be consulted by quoting a memorandum which Queen Victoria caused to be sent to Lord Palmerston, the Foreign Secretary, following Palmerston's cavalier handling of negotiations concerning the *coup d'état* of Louis Napoleon in 1851:

> The Queen requires, first, that Lord Palmerston will distinctly state what he proposes in a given case, in order that the Queen may know as distinctly to what she is giving her royal sanction. Secondly, having once given her sanction to such a measure that it be not arbitrarily altered or modified by the minister. Such an act she must consider as failing in sincerity towards the Crown, and justly to be visited by the exercise of her constitutional right of dismissing that minister.

A century later an American President[6] was writing to his Secretary of State in an identical vein:

> I received no communication from you directly while you were in Moscow. The only message I had from you came as a reply to one which I had Undersecretary Acheson send to you about my

[5] *Ibid.*, p. 66.
[6] Harry S Truman, *Year of Decisions,* Doubleday & Company, Inc., Garden City, N.Y., 1955, p. 551.

interview with the Senate Committee on Atomic Energy. . . . The protocol was not submitted to me, nor was the communiqué. I was completely in the dark on the whole conference until I requested you to come to the *Williamsburg* and inform me. The communiqué was released before I ever saw it.

The removal of General MacArthur is one of the more dramatic episodes illustrating the right to be consulted in recent American history.[7] On June 25, 1950, North Korean forces began the invasion of the Republic of Korea. The same day the United Nations Security Council branded the invasion a breach of the peace, and demanded the immediate cessation of hostilities. The demand was ignored. On June 27, 1950, the Security Council defined the North Koreans as the aggressors, and requested member states to supply armed forces for resisting the aggression and restoring peace. On July 27, 1950, the Security Council requested all member states supplying armed forces to put them under the unified command of the United States.

At this time Gen. Douglas MacArthur was in Tokyo, a short distance to the south of Korea, as supreme commander of the Allied forces occupying Japan and as commanding general of American forces in the Far East. In response to the United Nations resolution of June 25, Truman gave MacArthur and his forces the responsibility for United States military assistance to Korea. Under the United Nations resolution of July 27, requesting the United States to take charge of the collective security operation, Truman appointed MacArthur United Nations field commander.

The policy of the United Nations and of the United States was to confine the conflict, to restore the *status quo* at the time the invasion began, and to avoid actions which might enlarge its scope. To this end it had neutralized Formosa in the early days of the war, interposing the Seventh Fleet between the island and the mainland. Early in August Truman sent Averell Harriman to convey to the general the President's specific instruction that Chiang must not be permitted to start a war with the Chinese Communists on the mainland. Harriman recorded that the general said he would accept whatever orders the President gave him but reported that MacArthur's reply was "without full conviction."

[7] A good general account of the incident may be found in John W. Spanier's *The Truman-MacArthur Controversy and the Korean War* (Belknap Press of the Harvard University Press, Cambridge, Mass., 1959).

In late August the general's lack of full conviction became more apparent. In a statement sent to the commander of the Veterans of Foreign Wars MacArthur called, in effect, for a military policy of aggression, based upon Formosa's position. At the direction of the President, Secretary of Defense Johnson sent MacArthur a message on August 26 instructing him to withdraw his statement because in its references to Formosa it was in conflict with the foreign policy of the United States and its position in the United Nations. General Mac-Arthur withdrew the statement, although the text had already been released to the press, and was printed in full in a national weekly magazine.

The President then wrote MacArthur a long personal letter, explaining to him the rationale of the diplomatic position, the necessity of confining military operations to Korea, and the importance of avoiding any extension of hostilities to other theaters. Two weeks later Mac-Arthur's troops landed at Inchon, and before the end of September had liberated Seoul and reached the boundary between North and South Korea at the 38th parallel. On October 2 he reported that Republic of Korea troops were operating north of the parallel and encountering little enemy resistance. However, the Chinese Communists had called in the Indian Ambassador to Peiping and told him that if United Nations troops crossed the parallel the Red Chinese would come into the war, but that if Republic of Korea troops alone crossed the parallel Red China would take no action. This information was communicated to MacArthur, and the Joint Chiefs instructed him with respect to his authorities in the event major Chinese Communist units were encountered. Truman flew to meet the general at Wake Island, and spent Sunday, October 15, in conference with him. MacArthur assured the President that the victory was already won in Korea, that the Chinese Communists would not attack, that all resistance would end by Thanksgiving, and that "the boys would be home by Christmas."

The general's intelligence was tragically deficient. The next day organized Chinese units crossed the Yalu. By October 26 they were in contact with the X Corps in the Wonson sector. On December 3 MacArthur reported that the Reds had 26 divisions in the line and 200,000 men in reserve. On January 1 Seoul fell to the Communists. MacArthur retreated two-thirds of the way down the peninsula, and for some weeks it was doubtful whether he could retain a foothold in Korea at all. In the face of military adversity the general announced the coming of a "new war," returned to his advocacy of all-out military action against the Chinese Communists, and in a communiqué of November 6 by implication blamed Washington for his troubles because he was not permitted to attack the ammunition dumps, supply depots, and reserve concentrations of the Chinese beyond the Yalu River, which formed the boundary between Korea and Red China. He publicly referred to Washington's refusal to let him go to war with Peiping as "extraordinary inhibitions . . . without precedent in military history." The President issued an order prohibiting speeches, press releases, or other public statements concerning foreign policy without prior clearance with the State Department.

General Ridgeway, commanding the ground forces in Korea, was of the opinion that South Korea could be cleared of the Communists without running the risk of all-out war with Peiping and perhaps the Soviet Union as well. By March his military operations were demonstrating the feasibility of his plan of campaign. But MacArthur apparently regarded any solution of the conflict which did not exact retribution for the lese majesty of the Reds in driving him almost off the peninsula as tantamount to surrender. On March 24 he issued a remarkable communiqué which, in effect, called for unconditional surrender and implied a threat to throw the full power of the United Nations forces against Red China. This, of course, was diametrically opposed to United Nations and United States policy. The Joint Chiefs, on order of the President, reminded the general that his ukases were required to be cleared with the State Department. The President thought the matter over for several days, and decided, in the measured words of Queen Victoria, that the general's acts must be considered as failing in sincerity toward the Presidency, and were justly to be visited by the exercise of the President's constitutional right to dismiss him.

The dismissal of MacArthur was no petulant assertion of *amourpropre* by the Commander in Chief. The stakes were tremendous. They were nothing less than our entire strategic aim in conducting the war. The question was whether our leadership of the police action in Korea was to be utilized to sustain the aims of the United Nations and the United States in redressing the imbalance produced by North Korean and subsequently Red Chinese aggression and restoring the rule of law, or whether the desire of some Americans, of whom MacArthur was one, for a showdown with the Communists should lead us into what the Chairman of the Joint Chiefs of Staff rightly called the wrong war, in the wrong place, at the wrong time, against the wrong enemy. In a larger sense, the issue was the position of the United States as a moral leader of the free world, and as the major protagonist of the rule of law in the community of nations.

THE RIGHT TO ENCOURAGE

Much of what has been called the aggrandizement of presidential power is in fact the expansion of the President's right to encourage. Bagehot[8] speaks of the right to encourage in these words:

> . . . a wise and great constitutional monarch . . . labors in the world of sober fact; he deals with schemes which can be effected—schemes which are desirable—schemes which are worth the cost. He says to the ministry . . . "I think so and so; do you see if there is anything in it. I have put down my reasons in a certain memorandum, which I will give you. Probably it does not exhaust the subject, but it will suggest materials for your consideration. . . ."

President Truman said almost the same thing in a somewhat different way: "I sit here all day trying to persuade people to do the things they ought to have sense enough to do without my persuading them. . . . That's all the powers of the President amount to."[9]

In his address to Congress on the Greek-Turkish Aid program on March 12, 1947, the President of the United States[10] spoke in part as follows:

> I believe that it must be the policy of the United States to support free peoples who are resisting attempted subjugation by armed minorities or by outside pressures.
>
> I believe that we must assist free peoples to work out their destiny in their own way.
>
> I believe that our help should be primarily through economic and financial aid, which is essential to economic stability and orderly political processes.

[8] *Op. cit.*, p. 72.
[9] Quoted in Richard E. Neustadt, *Presidential Power*, John Wiley & Sons, Inc., New York, 1960, pp. 9–10.
[10] Joseph M. Jones, *The Fifteen Weeks*, The Viking Press, Inc., New York, 1955, p. 22. This book gives a full account of the genesis and development of the Marshall Plan.

By May, 1947, it was evident that our postwar economic planners had grossly underestimated the actual destruction to productive facilities during the war. They had underestimated the damage done to the infrastructure of the European economy and society, in the form of the breakdown of basic economic and commercial motivation in the European countries. They had underestimated the depths and pervasiveness of political and social demoralization which followed in the wake of the war.

The President's approach to the Greek-Turkish Aid program had encouraged the Secretary of State, George Catlett Marshall, to try to put together a proposal that would be responsive to the steady deterioration of the European economy and the growing influence of Communism in Western Europe. In one of the most portentous speeches of our era, delivered at the commencement exercises of Harvard University June 5, 1947, the Secretary of State told his audience:

> The truth of the matter is that Europe's requirements for the next three or four years of foreign food and other essential products—principally from America—are so much greater than her present ability to pay that she must have substantial additional help or face economic, social and political deterioration of a very grave character. The remedy lies in breaking the vicious circle and restoring the confidence of the European people in the economic future of their own countries and of Europe as a whole.

In the early summer of 1947 the executive branch was presided over by a man generally regarded as a caretaker President. Truman had just finished his second tempestuous year since Roosevelt's death had catapulted him into the White House in April, 1945. In the elections the prior November the President's party had lost control of both Houses of Congress, breaking an uninterrupted reign of 14 years. The President's lack of popularity with the Republicans was equaled only by his lack of popularity with large numbers of Democrats. Almost everyone —except the President himself—was certain that he would be out of office in 18 months. A senator of his own party had gone so far as to suggest that the President appoint a Republican Secretary of State, under the then Succession Act next in line, and resign. Robert Taft, the Republican leader in the Senate, was so sure of the shape of things to come that he had already assumed the presidential toga. To cap the climax, the President was to veto within a fortnight after Marshall's address at Cambridge the two major achievements of the new Republican congressional majority—the Taft-Hartley Labor Relations Bill and income-tax reduction.

Moreover, the President's own administrative family was a house divided. The Treasury, intent upon a balanced budget, was not enthusiastic about the huge commitments of foreign economic aid implicit in the European Recovery Program. The Defense establishment, smarting under drastic reductions in expenditure authorization and virtually disarmed by sustained cutbacks, looked askance upon a "giveaway" program for spending money abroad that the Pentagon felt it could invest much better in behalf of the national security at home. Domestic agencies, pressing for the expansion of social security, housing, Federal aid to education, and various other welfare operations did not welcome competition before the appropriations committees.

Ten months after Marshall spoke at Harvard the European Recovery Act had been passed, Paul Hoffman had been named Administrator, the machinery of execution was in being, and the funds for the first year of the program were in sight. A policy innovation of this magnitude within so short a period by any American President not literally confronted with a major national emergency would have been an event of the first order of importance. That it was achieved at all in the face of the untoward conditions of the time raises its status to that of an extraordinary feat of political legerdemain. And that it was accomplished by a caretaker President merely waiting, it was supposed, to go back home to Independence converted it into an authentic minor miracle. As things turned out, of course, the President was not waiting to go home at all, but at the time this was not generally understood.

Part of the secret of the President's success in this exercise of the right to encourage resides in the unusual quality of his first team at the time. George Marshall was not only a great administrator and an extraordinarily able Secretary of State, but as wartime Chairman of the Joint Chiefs of Staff was more than any other one person responsible for the military victory of the United Nations. Associated with Marshall were men such as Dean Acheson, Robert Lovett, and Will Clayton.

But the President could not have succeeded with Marshall and his collaborators alone. There was every reason for the Republican leadership in Congress to delay action until the President's scheduled departure from the White House at the beginning of 1949, at which time it could, if circumstances required, enact a "Vandenberg" plan and reap the credit itself. In his way, Vandenberg occupied a position on the Hill very much like that of Marshall at the other end of Pennsylvania Avenue. He had been a senator for two decades, was Chairman of the Senate Committee on Foreign Relations and the senior member of his party in the Chamber. Despite his unconcealed distaste for Franklin D. Roosevelt and for Truman, he was the chief proponent of bipartisanship in foreign policy. Under Vandenberg's leadership in 1947 the Republican majorities were prepared to pursue responsible policies in what they regarded as the twilight of the Truman administration, and to demonstrate to the country their ability to put patriotism above party. Vandenberg was not the only man in Congress to respond to the President's encouragement, and he drove some hard bargains with Truman as the price of the encouragement he was willing to receive, but he did cooperate, and he did carry his party with him.

It is important to remember that the President, in his speech on the Greek-Turkish Aid program, had said, "I believe that we must assist free peoples to work out their destiny *in their own way*." At Harvard, Marshall had emphasized that planning for economic recovery in Europe ". . . is the business of Europeans." Ernest Bevan, the British Foreign Secretary, was sufficiently encouraged by these statements that, in concert with the leaders of other European nations, he organized a European response to the Marshall Plan proposals so amply and concretely that it not only exceeded the President's fondest expectations but embarrassed the United States government by its promptness.

The U.S.S.R. and the then members of the Soviet bloc were invited to become a part of the recovery program. The Russians and their satellites attended the Paris meetings, in the course of which Molotov sought to exhibit his contempt for the effort by a dramatic walkout. When Czechoslovakia, at that time still independent, continued to show interest in the Marshall Plan, a Communist coup in February, 1948, overturned the Prague government under the protective wing of Soviet military concentrations poised on the nearby frontier. Thirty days later the Marshall Plan was approved by the Congress.

THE RIGHT TO WARN

Bagehot[11] writes of the English monarch's right to warn in these words:

> [The monarch] would say to his minister: "The responsibility of these measures is upon you. Whatever

[11] *Op. cit.*, p. 67.

you think best must be done. Whatever you think best shall have my full and effectual support. *But you will observe that for this reason and that reason what you propose to do is bad; for this reason and that reason what you do not propose is better.* I do not oppose it, it is my duty not to oppose; but observe that I warn."

The President of the United States, unlike the English monarch, is under a very strong and highly specific obligation with respect to the right to warn. The President, not the minister, is answerable for all the acts of his administration, and he is never in a position to say to a member of his Cabinet, "The responsibility of these measures is upon you." The right to warn, therefore, is a much more important component of presidential leadership in the United States than it is of the leadership of the monarch in the United Kingdom.

The right to warn is used in many ways. One of its most dramatic institutional manifestations is the veto power given to the President in Article I, section 7, of the Constitution, which enables him to return bills to the Congress with his disapproval, which unless reenacted by a two-thirds vote of each house, do not become law. But he also warns people other than those in Congress. He warns the American people, as Washington did in 1789 on the maintenance of neutrality in the war between England and France. He warns foreign nations, as President Monroe did in 1823 when he proclaimed the Monroe Doctrine advising European nations not to seek territorial expansion in the Western Hemisphere. He warns the Congress by means other than the veto, as Franklin D. Roosevelt did in 1942 when he sent the Hill an ultimatum on the amendment of the Emergency Price Control Act. And sometimes, as Franklin D. Roosevelt did in his Supreme Court reorganization plan of 1937, he warns the judiciary.

A spectacular example of the importance of the President's right to warn occurred in 1832 during the administration of Andrew Jackson, when South Carolina sought to nullify the tariff acts passed by the United States Congress in 1828 and 1832. On this occasion Jackson issued a stern admonition to the people of South Carolina and the officials of the South Carolina state government, to the people of the United States, and to the Congress. His warning, moreover, was not merely verbal; he took executive action at the same time which demonstrated quite clearly that he meant what he said.

In November, 1832, the very month in which President Jackson had won reelection, a constitutional convention assembled by the South Carolina Legislature passed an ordinance not only declaring the tariff acts of 1828 and 1832 "null, void, and no law, nor binding upon this State, its officers or citizens," but also that "all judicial proceedings which shall be hereafter had in affirmance thereof, are and shall be held utterly null and void."[12] It proclaimed, moreover, that it should be unlawful for any state or Federal authorities to attempt to enforce payments under the two tariff acts within the territorial limits of South Carolina, and that the South Carolina Legislature should adopt such legislation as might be necessary to prevent the enforcement of the tariff acts in the state.

This action presented the President with a very interesting question: Could a state set aside acts of the national government which it deemed to infringe upon its rights and liberties? Jackson thought it could not, but he was in a difficult position to do anything about it. He could send troops into South Carolina or any other state at the request of the Governor—an unlikely event in this instance—or to see to it that the laws enacted by Congress were faithfully executed. But legislation covering the latter point contemplated only violations by individuals; there was no provision that dealt with violations by the duly constituted public authorities. Since he could not use the Army, his only remaining recourse was the *posse comitatus*—the voluntary troop of private citizens commissioned by law enforcement officers to assist in dealing with a specific incident, familiar to all confirmed television viewers. The *posse* was a wholly legal, but incredibly awkward, method of coping with nullification.

In his fourth annual message to Congress early in December Jackson reported on the nullification crisis in South Carolina. On December 10 he issued his famous proclamation, directed to the people of the United States including South Carolina, in which he said, among other things:

> The ordinance is founded . . . on the strange position . . . that the true construction of that instrument [the Constitution] permits a State to retain its place in the Union and yet be bound by no other of its laws than those it may choose to consider as constitutional. . . . I consider . . . the power to annul a law of the United States, assumed by one State, *in-*

[12] George Fort Milton, *The Use of Presidential Power*, Little, Brown and Company, Boston, 1944, p. 90 et seq. This book contains an account of the nullification crisis.

> *compatible with the existence of the Union, contra-*
> *dicted expressly by the letter of the Constitution,*
> *unauthorized by its spirit, inconsistent with every*
> *principle on which it was founded and destructive*
> *of the great object for which it was formed.* . . . On
> such expositions and reasonings the ordinance grounds
> not only an assertion of the right to annul the laws
> of which it complains, but to enforce it by a threat
> of seceding from the Union if any attempt is made
> to execute them. . . . Disunion by armed force is
> *treason.*

The proclamation drew warm support from both state governments and citizens from Maine to Louisiana, and by the date on which the nullification ordinance was to have entered into force (February 1, 1833) Jackson could have put a *posse comitatus* of more than two hundred thousand men in the field.

Simultaneously with the issuance of the proclamation, the President caused to be introduced in Congress legislation authorizing the use of the Army against the state authorities. He also alerted the substantial body of South Carolina Unionists, who were bitterly opposed to the nullification ordinance, to prepare for overt acts of nullification. He gathered arms for their use, and sent several naval vessels to Charleston Harbor, where he put Gen. Winfield Scott in command. The effective date of the nullification ordinance passed, but no overt act of nullification occurred.

Senators Clay and Calhoun were meanwhile at work in the Senate drafting a compromise tariff bill with the aim of saving face, to some degree, for the nullificationists, which provided over a period of ten years for gradual tariff reduction. The senators secured support for their measure in the House, and by adroit maneuvering succeeded in putting the compromise tariff measure ahead of the President's armed forces bill on the House calendar. Both bills emerged March 2, 1833. The South Carolina convention promptly convened, repealed the tariff act ordinance, and passed another ordinance nullifying the applicability of the President's armed forces act in South Carolina. It then proclaimed itself the indisputable victor in the contest with the President and dissolved. Nevertheless, the tariff acts were enforced, in South Carolina precisely as in the rest of the country. There was no disorder. There was no secession. And the people of the United States were under no misconception as to who won.

Review Questions

1. What have been the major influences in the expansion of the power of the President?

2. Has the growth of presidential power been beneficial or detrimental to the national welfare? Give your reasons.

3. Make a list of the activities of the President reported by one of the national weekly news magazines for the past three months, and classify the reported activities accordingly as they represent the exercise of the President's right to be consulted, his right to encourage, and his right to warn. Give the reasons for your classification.

4. What did Bagehot mean by "the right to be consulted"? What does this concept mean as applied to the American Presidency? If you think the concepts have different meanings in England and in the United States, what produces the difference?

5. In what specific ways did General MacArthur disregard the President's right to be consulted? Can you think of other incidents in American history in which important Federal officials have disregarded the President's right to be consulted?

6. In what particulars is the President's "right to encourage" broader than that of the British sovereign? In what respects is it narrower?

7. In what specific ways did President Truman use his right to encourage in securing the drafting and the enactment of the Marshall Plan?

8. What is meant by "the right to warn"? What specific actions of President Jackson in the nullification controversy illustrate the exercise of the right to warn?

9. Do you think the essential nature of the American Presidency is more clearly understood by conceiving of the President as an "elective king" or as the general manager of a corporation? Why is one concept better than the other?

PRESIDENTIAL LEADERSHIP

Chapter 2

THE PRESIDENT AS
CHIEF EXECUTIVE

Although the Constitution vests in a single person "the executive power," the President obviously cannot himself execute all the laws. The framers were aware of this, and consequently limited his obligation to taking care that the laws be faithfully executed. The essential problem of the President as Chief Executive is to establish and maintain that degree of control over the entire executive establishment which is necessary to insure its unity and integrity, and permit him the certainty that the laws are in fact being faithfully executed.

Control of the executive establishment derives primarily from the President's powers of appointment and removal, and from the power of administrative direction. Article II, section 2, of the Constitution reads in part:

> [The President] shall nominate, and by and with the advice and consent of the Senate, shall appoint ambassadors, other public ministers and consuls, judges of the Supreme Court, and all other officers of the United States, whose appointments are not herein otherwise provided for, and which shall be established by law; but the Congress may by law vest the appointment of such inferior officers, as they think proper, in the President alone, in the courts of law, or in the heads of departments.

The power of appointment is thus defined with some clarity in the Constitution, and in the course of history has been much broadened by congressional action vesting the appointment of inferior officers—and some not so inferior, such as the Director of the Budget—in the President alone. The appointing power of the courts has been restricted to inferior officers of the judicial branch. The President is, in fact, usually consulted about appointments vested by law in the heads of the executive departments and agencies.

But the power to remove is an even more important element of presidential control than the power to appoint. And on this point the Constitution is strangely silent. In 1789 the First Congress was confronted with the necessity of setting up the executive departments. Who should have the power to remove department heads? Only a few members of the House, where the legislation originated, contended that impeachment and conviction of high crimes and misdemeanors should be the only way of dismissing government officials. A small minority thought that since the advice and consent of the Senate was necessary for appointment it should likewise be a part of the removal process. James Madison, who was to become the fourth President, was then a member of the House. He enunciated the view destined to prevail in one of the classics of constitutional history:[1]

> If the President should possess alone the power of removal from office, those who are employed in the execution of the law will be in their proper situa-

[1] *Annals*, 1st Cong., 1789–1791, cols. 518–519.

tion, and the chain of dependency be preserved; the lowest officers, the middle grade and the highest, will depend, as they ought, on the President, and the President on the community. . . . Take the other supposition; that the power should be vested in the Senate, on the principle that the power to displace is necessarily connected with the power to appoint. It is declared by the Constitution, that we may by law vest the appointment of inferior officers in the heads of departments; the power of removal being incidental, as stated by some gentlemen. Where does this terminate? If you begin with the subordinate officers, they are dependent on their superior, he on the next superior, and he on—whom? On the Senate, . . . Instead of keeping the departments of government distinct, you make an Executive out of one branch of the Legislature; you make the Executive a two-headed monster, . . . you destroy the great principle of responsibility, and perhaps have the creature divided in its will, defeating the very purpose for which a unity in the Executive was instituted.

The President's removal power has been attacked from time to time by the Congress, notably in the tenure of office legislation enacted in 1867 and amended in 1869. Although these acts, which were in force for twenty years, were never subjected to judicial test, the Court's decision in 1926 in *Myers v. United States* indicates quite clearly that they were in fact unconstitutional. The position urged by Madison unquestionably states the rule with respect to officers performing essentially executive duties.

The powers of the President are derived in part from the Constitution, and in part from the statutes. A few of his constitutional powers must be exercised by him personally, but the routine exercise of his constitutional diplomatic and command powers, and almost all of his statutory powers may be legally, and must be practically, carried out under his direction by the responsible heads of departments and administrative agencies. Heads of departments in exercising presidential powers, from whatever source derived, must obviously be subject to his direction and hence liable to removal by the President at his discretion.

The powers of heads of departments and agencies, on the other hand, are wholly statutory. There is no reference anywhere in the Constitution to departments, and the whole of the executive power under the Constitution is given to the President. The organic legislation of 1789 charged the Secretary of State, for example, with the execution of the duties enjoined upon him by the President in the field of foreign affairs. Similarly, the Secretary of War was charged with the duties enjoined upon him by the President in the field of military and naval affairs. Since the President is, under the Constitution, the only channel for the conduct of foreign relations as well as the Commander in Chief, both of these officers are involved in exercising constitutional powers of the President. The 1789 legislation on the Secretary of the Treasury, however, was somewhat different; the duties it imposed related to supervising the collection of the revenue, prescribing accounting forms, issuing warrants for the expenditure of public funds, controlling the sale of public lands, etc. None of these duties impinged upon the President's constitutional powers except insofar as he was responsible for seeing that the laws, including the revenue and other laws, were faithfully executed.

This raised the question whether the duty of the Secretary of the Treasury was to the President or to the congressional statutes. The issue came sharply into focus in 1833 in the great controversy over the Bank of the United States. Andrew Jackson, the President, was a bitter and implacable enemy of the Bank. Its restrictive credit policies had caused great hardship among the "western" farmers in Tennessee and Kentucky; indeed, Jackson had himself been a victim of the Bank's hard-money bias. Shortly before the election of 1832, Henry Clay introduced in Congress a bill for the renewal of the charter of the Bank. The Bank of the United States was a private bank in which all United States government funds were deposited, interest free, and these deposits were the source of its massive influence on money and credit policies. Clay's bill was passed, although the Bank's charter was not at the point of expiring, and President Jackson vetoed it.

Jackson's ultimate objective was the disestablishment of the Bank. Since its charter still had several years to run, however, he attempted to break the Bank's control of interest rates by withdrawing United States government funds and depositing them in selected banks operating under state charters. Jackson's problem was to get the Secretary of the Treasury to exercise his discretion, under the Bank's charter, in such a way as to remove government deposits from the Bank. Louis

McLane, Secretary of the Treasury at the time of Jackson's reelection, was known to oppose the removal of the deposits. Jackson transferred him to the Department of State. McLane was succeeded by William J. Duane, who took the oath of office on June 1, 1833. Two days later in an interview with the President the new Secretary expressed misgivings about the removal of the deposits and suggested that Congress be asked to inquire into the matter. Jackson, however, had no intention of battling with the President of the Bank, Nicholas Biddle, in the halls of Congress.

A rapid sequence of correspondence and conversations quickly brought the President and Duane to an impasse. In letters written to Duane on June 26, 1833, Jackson explained in detail his views and policies with respect to the Bank. Duane undertook an inquiry into the use of state banks as depositories, and in his draft of instructions on the inquiry implied that even if the outcome of the study were favorable he would not feel himself at liberty to carry into effect a decision to transfer government funds to them. Jackson advised Duane that if he had correctly interpreted Duane's views, it would then become the President's duty to suggest to the Secretary the course of action which would be necessary on the part of the President. Duane replied, in effect, that he would resign if, after concluding his inquiry, he still felt unable to carry out the President's decision.

Duane continued his inquiries and exchanges with the President. On September 18, 1833, Jackson presented a paper to the Cabinet in which he reaffirmed his intention of transferring government deposits from the Bank of the United States to the state banks, and developed in some detail his views of the relation of the Secretary of the Treasury to the President in the matter. Three days later Duane told the President he could not transfer the deposits. Duane had somewhere in the course of the negotiations forgotten his promise to resign, and confronted with both his unwillingness to carry out the President's decision and his unwillingness to leave, Jackson wrote him a note saying, "I feel myself constrained to notify you that your further services as Secretary of the Treasury are no longer required." Attorney General, later Chief Justice, Roger B. Taney was appointed Secretary of the Treasury on September 23, and the government deposits transferred forthwith.

On March 28, 1834, Senator Clay offered a Resolution of Censure in the Senate "That the President, in the late Executive proceedings in relation to the public revenue, has assumed upon himself authority and power not conferred by the constitution and laws, but in derogation of both." Jackson thereupon presented a protest, which the Senate declined to receive. In the protest, after a review of the antecedents, he reiterated his view of the President's power of administrative direction:[2]

> Thus was it settled by the Constitution, the laws, and the whole practice of the Government that the entire executive power is vested in the President of the United States; that as incident to that power the right of appointing and removing those officers who are to aid him in the execution of the laws, with such restrictions only as the Constitution prescribes, is vested in the President; that the Secretary of the Treasury is one of those officers; that the custody of the public property and money is an Executive function which, in relation to the money, has always been exercised through the Secretary of the Treasury and his subordinates; that in the performance of these duties he is subject to the supervision and control of the President, and in all important measures having relation to them consults the Chief Magistrate and obtains his approval and sanction; that the law establishing the Bank did not, as it could not, change the relation between the President and the Secretary—did not release the former from his obligation to see the law faithfully executed nor the latter from the President's supervision and control.

Senator Benton, following the Senate's refusal to consider the President's protest, gave notice of his intention to expunge the censure, and by 1837 had obtained the necessary majority. The censure was formally expunged January 16, 1837. "Never before and never since," Professor Corwin has written, "has the Senate so abased itself before a President."[3] But more than the President's honor was at stake. The Duane affair settled once and for all the legal, as well as the *de facto*, existence of

---

[2] James D. Richardson, *A Compilation of the Messages and Papers of the Presidents, 1789–1910* (Apr. 15, 1834), vol. III, p. 85, reprinted by the Bureau of National Literature, 1917.

[3] Edward S. Corwin, *The President: Office and Powers*, New York University Press, New York, 1940, p. 267.

a plenary power of administrative direction in the President. There would be no doubt from 1833 on that the President is the Chief Executive in the broadest sense of the term.

THE PRESIDENT AS CHIEF ADMINISTRATOR

The integrity of the executive branch of the government is, as mentioned before, assured by the President's powers of appointment, removal, and administrative direction. But these are merely the preconditions of coordinated administrative action. The vast and complex business of the government goes on day in and day out in an atmosphere far removed from the dramatic episodes of a Duane affair or a Myers case. Many aspects of government business the President touches only infrequently, and some of them he touches hardly at all. Even his own constitutional and statutory powers are exercised personally only when from their nature, from the intent of the framers, or from their impact generally throughout the government, the exercise of his own judgment is essential. When he does act personally, his action is usually taken upon the advice of administrative subordinates.

At the same time the acts of the President's subordinates are in the contemplation of the law his acts. They are likewise his acts in the eyes of the Congress and the country. If as a practical matter there must be an enormous amount of devolution of decision preparing and decision making, it is equally true that the responsibility of the President for the acts of his subordinates must be safeguarded by the maintenance of continuous access by the President to the mainstream of policy formulation and administrative action throughout the government. The maintenance of this access is the process which is called administrative management. In its simplest term this implies three things. First, he must systematize the exercise of his right to be consulted, so that he does not merely react to problems which happen fortuitously to reach his desk, but anticipates them, assures himself that he is consulted when he should be consulted, and provides himself with machinery for handling on his behalf and under his general direction problems that are of a recurring nature. Second, he must provide himself with facilities for making critical judgments of the proposals and recommendations offered by the heads of departments and agencies—as Franklin D. Roosevelt called it, "triangulating" upon their advice—so that he is not at the mercy of a particular interest or point of view. Third, he must maintain his ability to dip down into the flow of policy formulation and action in the departments and agencies on his own motion, in order to call up novel or politically critical questions, through continuing participation in certain processes of departmental and agency management.

Since the President is only one man, and, however brilliant, has limited knowledge and no more hours in his day than anyone else, he can maintain continuing supervision over the departments and agencies only if he is staffed. The history of the Presidency, until recent years, has been one of niggardliness and inadequacy in the provision of staff assistance. Until 1857 Congress made no provision even for clerical assistance to the President. In that year funds were appropriated for a private secretary, a steward to supervise the housekeeping in the Executive Mansion, and a messenger. Except for a few additional clerks this was substantially the manning table of the President's office until President Hoover in 1928 was authorized to increase the number of secretaries to three. Outside the White House two agencies had been created which provided certain staff assistance to the President. The Civil Service Commission was established in 1883 as a bipartisan board to police the appointment and removal of classified employees. The Bureau of the Budget was created in 1921 to prepare the annual budget; it was under the President's general control, but was located administratively in the Treasury Department.

In 1939 President Roosevelt initiated the process that was to eventuate in the Executive Office of the President, in which were assembled and systematically organized a substantial part of the staff organization through which the processes of administrative management are carried out. In 1937 the President's Committee on Administrative Management urged the establishment of an Executive Office and the strengthening and development as auxiliaries to the President of the managerial agencies of the government as well as the expansion of the White House staff. Action on the recommendations of the committee had been blocked by congressional reaction to the President's so-called "Supreme Court packing" proposal, as well as by the traditional inability of Congress to pass reorganization legislation. In 1939, however, Congress itself developed a formula to overcome its difficulties in dealing with administrative reorganization; this formula consisted in giving the President authority to lay before Congress reorganization plans which within 60 days after submission became law unless rejected by concurrent resolution passed by both houses. Under this authority the President on April 25, 1939, for the first time in history, gave official countenance to the Executive Office in the following excerpt from Reorganization Plan I:

> The Bureau of the Budget and all its functions and personnel (including the Director and Assistant Director) are hereby transferred from the Treasury Department to the Executive Office of the President; and the functions of the Bureau of the Budget shall be administered by the Director thereof under the supervision and direction of the President.

The same plan transferred the National Resources Planning Board to the Executive Office of the President and the Central Statistical Board to the Bureau of the Budget. Later in the year the structure and functions of the Executive Office were elaborated in Executive Order 8248, which read in part as follows:

> I
>
> There shall be within the Executive Office of the President the following principal divisions, namely: (1) the White House Office, (2) the Bureau of the Budget, (3) the National Resources Planning Board; (4) the Liaison Office for Personnel Management; (5) the Office of Government Reports, and (6) in the event of a national emergency, or threat of a national emergency, such office for emergency management as the President shall determine.
>
> II
>
> The functions and duties of the divisions of the Executive Office of the President are hereby defined as follows:
>
> 1. *The White House Office.*—In general, to serve the President in an intimate capacity in the performance of the many detailed activities incident to his immediate office. To that end the White House Office shall be composed of the following principal subdivisions, with particular functions and duties as indicated: . . .
>
> 2. *The Bureau of the Budget.*—(*a*) to assist the President in the preparation of the Budget and the formation of the fiscal program of the Government.

(*b*) To supervise and control administration of the Budget.

(*c*) To conduct research in the development of improved plans of administrative management, and to advise the executive departments and agencies of the Government with respect to improved administrative organization and practice.

(*d*) To aid the President to bring about more efficient and economical conduct of government service.

(*e*) To assist the President by clearing and coordinating departmental advice on proposed legislation and by making recommendations as to Presidential action on legislative enactments, in accordance with past practice.

(*f*) To assist in the consideration and clearance and, where necessary, in the preparation of proposed Executive orders and proclamations, in accordance with the provisions of Executive Order No. 7298 of February 18, 1936.

(*g*) To plan and promote the improvement, development, and coordination of Federal and other statistical services.

(*h*) To keep the President informed of the progress of activities by agencies of the government with respect to work proposed, work actually initiated, and work completed, together with the relative timing of work between the several agencies of the government; all to the end that the work programs of the several agencies of the Executive branch of the government may be coordinated and that the monies appropriated by the Congress may be expended in the most economical manner possible with the least possible overlapping and duplication of effort. . . .

The Executive Office of the President has undergone many changes since Executive Order 8248 was promulgated, and it will doubtless undergo many others in the future. At the present time (1962) it is made up of: (1) the White House Office, (2) the Bureau of the

Budget, (3) the National Security Council, (4) the Council of Economic Advisers, (5) the Office of Emergency Planning, (6) the Central Intelligence Agency, (7) the National Aeronautics and Space Council, and (8) the Office of Science and Technology.

THE PRESIDENT AND FOREIGN POLICY

The primacy of the President in the field of foreign affairs is assured by the fact that he is the only channel of official intercourse between the United States government and the governments of foreign nations. There is nothing in the Constitution, however, that explicitly makes the President the sole medium of official international relations of the United States. The only-channel doctrine is an inference from the language of the framers, but it is an inference which has been taken for granted since the beginning of the Republic.

The initial enunciation of the only-channel doctrine was made in 1790, only a year after President Washington took office, by the then Secretary of State Thomas Jefferson. At that time when the President accredited an envoy to a foreign country he not only selected the person for whose appointment he solicited the advice and consent of the Senate, but he established the grade in accordance with the usages of the law of nations. The question arose whether the Senate might not negative the grade as well as the man. Jefferson's report to Washington read in part as follows: [4]

> The transaction of business with foreign nations is executive altogether; it belongs, then, to the head of that department, except as to such portions of it as are specifically submitted to the senate. Exceptions are to be construed strictly; the constitution itself, indeed, has taken care to circumscribe this one within very strict limits; for it gives the nomination of a foreign agent to the president, the appointment to him and the senate jointly, and the commissioning to the president.

The only-channel doctrine was considerably strengthened three years later in what Madison described as "the war between the Ex and Genet." M. Genet, the French minister in the United States, questioned

[4] Andrew A. Lipscomb and Albert Ellery Bergh (eds.), *The Writings of Thomas Jefferson*, Thomas Jefferson Memorial Association, 1905, vol. V, pp. 161–162.

the President's authority in certain matters in which his country was interested, and even threatened to appeal his case to Congress and to the people. Secretary of State Jefferson thereupon had a talk with Citizen Genet, which he reported to Washington as follows:[5]

> [Genet said] that to such propositions such a return ought not to have been made by the executive, without consulting Congress; and that, on the return of the President, he would certainly press him to convene Congress. He had by this time got into a moderate tone, and I stopped him on the subject of calling Congress, explained our Constitution to him, as having divided the functions of government among three different authorities, the executive, legislative, and judiciary, each of which were supreme in all questions belonging to their departments, and independent of the others; that all the questions, which had arisen between him and us, belonged to the executive department, and, if Congress were sitting, could not be carried to them, nor would they take any notice of them.

It is one thing to assert that the President is the only channel of official intercourse between the United States government and the governments of foreign nations. It is something quite different to argue that the President is in full and complete control of foreign policy. He is not. And therein resides one of the basic dilemmas of the American foreign policy process. The issue was confronted in 1793, and provoked one of the "great debates" of our constitutional history. But the essential dilemma remains unresolved.

On April 22, 1793, President Washington issued the following proclamation:[6]

> Whereas it appears that a state of war exists between Austria, Prussia, Sardinia, Great Britain, and the United Netherlands of the one part and France on the other, and the duty and interest of the United States require that they should with sincerity and good faith adopt and pursue a conduct friendly and impartial toward the belligerent powers:

[5] *Ibid.*, vol. I, p. 237.
[6] Richardson, *op. cit.*, vol. I, pp. 148–149.

> I have therefore thought fit by these presents to
> declare the disposition of the United States to ob-
> serve the conduct aforesaid toward those powers
> respectively, and to exhort and warn the citizens of
> the United States carefully to avoid all acts and pro-
> ceedings whatsoever which may in any manner tend
> to contravene such disposition.

Washington's policy of neutrality provoked deep controversy not
only in the country but within his own Cabinet, and the ensuing debate revealed for the first time the issues of political theory and constitutional law which to this day confuse the understanding of both
Americans and foreigners with respect to the foreign policy process.
Jefferson, Madison, and Monroe accepted the neutrality proclamation
as a warning to our own citizens of the existing legal situation. They
denied, however, the authority of the President to announce to the
belligerents a future policy of neutrality, and were acutely unhappy
with some of the language of the proclamation for that reason.

Hamilton, on the other hand, thought that the proclamation was a
declaration of neutrality and as such it was within the President's constitutional powers.[7] He argued that Article II of the Constitution,
which says that "The Executive Power shall be vested in a President
of the United States of America," provided a general grant of "the"
executive power of the nation to the President, and that this general
grant was restricted only by the qualifications and exceptions expressly
stipulated in the Constitution itself. Implicit in Hamilton's argument
was the assumption, quite correctly drawn from British precedent, that
war-declaring and treaty-making powers are executive in nature. Under
the British constitution, the Crown has the exclusive and unlimited
right to declare war and make treaties. The qualifications and limitations imposed upon those powers by the United States Constitution,
Hamilton thought, did not change the essential nature of the powers,
but merely altered the mode of their exercise.

Madison attacked this thesis, predicating as a major premise that the
essence of executive power was to assure the enforcement of preexisting
laws.[8] He then sought to demonstrate that the war-declaring and treaty-
making powers did not meet the requirements of the definition, but on

[7] John C. Hamilton (ed.), *The Works of Alexander Hamilton*, C. S. Francis
& Co., New York, 1851, vol. VII, pp. 77 et seq. and 112 et seq.
[8] Gaillard Hunt (ed.), *The Writings of James Madison*, G. P. Putnam's Sons,
New York, 1900–1910, vol. VI, pp. 138–151.

the contrary were more fundamentally akin to the making of laws. In *The Federalist* Hamilton had himself admitted that treaty making had more in common with the making of laws than with the execution of municipal legislation. But what Hamilton understood in this matter, and what Madison apparently did not, was that foreign relations partook of qualities and characteristics which were quite different from both the legislative and executive functions in purely domestic affairs.

Clearly, the fact that the President is the only channel of communication with foreign governments does not mean that the President necessarily has the final word with respect to what is communicated to them. The Senate may refuse, and in fact repeatedly has refused, to consent to treaties which the Executive has negotiated. Congress, through its powers of authorization and appropriation, frequently fixes the limits and defines the terms within which presidential policy must restrict itself. It is true, as Locke pointed out, that foreign relations cannot be conducted merely by passing a law, but it is equally true that much of contemporary international intercourse cannot be conducted without a law being passed. On the other hand, constitutional intent aside, the logic of events compels the spokesman of a nation in foreign relations to be more than a mere transmitter of legislative opinion. Foreign relations operate in a two-way street. The positions the United States assumes, and the actions it takes, frequently depend upon the positions and actions of other nations which are not under our control. If silence and inertia in the face of the pronouncements and actions of other nations are not to produce almost inevitable failure in the conduct of our foreign relations, the President's authority to speak more often than not becomes the authority to determine what is said. The President is, of course, subject in the pursuit of his foreign policies to the conditions and limitations imposed by Congress in the exercise of its constitutional powers and responsibilities. But the Congress is likewise subject to the facts of international life, which have been produced in large part by what the President has said and done, in exercising its own powers in the field of international affairs.

THE PRESIDENT AS COMMANDER IN CHIEF

If the Constitution creates a dilemma in the foreign-policy process as a result of the vagueness and ambiguity with which it allocates authority for the conduct of international relations, the dilemma created by the war-powers provisions is equally profound. Article II, section 2, paragraph 1 of the Constitution provides that "The President shall be Commander in Chief of the Army and Navy of the United States, and of the militia of the several States, when called into the actual Service of the United States. . . ." But Article I, section 8, paragraph 11 gives to Congress the power "To declare War, grant letters of Marque and Reprisal, and make Rules concerning Captures on Land and Water." Paragraphs 12 and 13 stipulate that Congress shall have the authority "To raise and support Armies. . . ." and "To provide and maintain a Navy." Paragraphs 14, 15, and 16 give Congress the power "To make rules for the Government and Regulation of the land and naval forces," "To provide for calling forth the Militia to execute the Laws of the Union, suppress Insurrections, and repel Invasions," and "To provide for organizing, arming, and disciplining the Militia, and for governing such Part of them as may be employed in the Service of the United States. . . ." Clearly, the President may be the Commander in Chief, but his powers are subject to check and restriction by Congress. That these competing claims in the sphere of the war powers have not resulted in catastrophic collision is doubtless due to the fact that the circumstances in which the powers are invoked have in the main been those in which the nation was closing ranks against grave national emergency, and the pressure of public opinion has left no room for intramural conflict.

It is possible to identify at least three principles in the pattern of distribution of the war powers which, if they do not reconcile the conflicting claims of presidential and congressional authority, at least establish some ground rules under which the contest is to be conducted. In the first place, the Constitution is quite explicit in giving to Congress the exclusive power to raise armies and establish a navy, and to regulate the general management and administration of the services in such detail as the Congress shall determine. In the second place, the President has the equally exclusive power of carrying out these statutory rules and regulations and of exercising military command in time of peace and in time of war; this command power, moreover, involves as an absolute minimum, upon which the Congress is powerless to encroach, the direction of military forces in combat and the military government of occupied enemy territory. In the third place, the President, as Commander in Chief, has concurrent power with the Congress, even without legal delegation from it, to issue orders and regulations not inconsistent with the rules established in legislation.

In the actual prosecution of military hostilities the President is in exclusive command of military operations. But he must depend upon Congress for the tools to do the job—for determining force levels, the numbers and kinds of ships, planes, ballistic missiles, and other weapons and armaments, for providing the money to acquire and use the men and the weapons, as well as for meeting the requirements of the home front in total war in respect of such things as economic stabilization, security against espionage and sabotage, and allocation of scarce resources.

In December, 1801, nine months after his inauguration, President Jefferson reported to the Congress in these words:[9]

> To this general state of peace with which we have been blessed, only one exception exists. Tripoli, the least considerable of the Barbary States, had come forward with demands unfounded either in right or in compact. . . . I sent a small squadron of frigates into the Mediterranean. . . . The Bey had already declared war. Our commerce in the Mediterranean was blockaded and that of the Atlantic in peril. The arrival of our squadron dispelled the danger. One of the Tripolitan cruisers was captured. . . . Unauthorized by the Constitution, without the sanction of Congress, to go beyond the line of defense, the vessel, being disabled from committing further hostilities, was liberated with its crew.

As was to be expected, Alexander Hamilton took exception to the position of President Jefferson, and in effect resumed the argument initiated some years before in connection with President Washington's neutrality proclamation. In his examination of the President's report on Tripoli, Hamilton wrote as follows:[10]

> War, of itself, gives to the parties a mutual right to kill in battle, and to capture the persons and property of each other. This is a rule of natural law; a necessary and inevitable consequence of the state of war. . . .
>
> It will be readily allowed, that the constitution of a particular country may limit the organ charged

[9] Richardson, *op. cit.*, vol. I, pp. 314–315.
[10] Henry Cabot Lodge (ed.), *The Works of Alexander Hamilton*, G. P. Putnam's Sons, New York, 1903, vol. VIII, p. 246 et seq.

with the direction of the public force, in the use or application of that force, even in time of actual war. Our Constitution, happily . . . has only provided affirmatively, that, "The Congress shall have power to declare war"; the plain meaning of which is, that it is the peculiar and exclusive province of Congress, *when the nation is at peace*, to change that state into a state of war; whether from calculations of policy, or from provocations or injuries received; in other words, it belongs to Congress only, *to go to war*. But when a foreign national declares or openly and avowedly makes war upon the United States, they are then by the very fact *already at war*, and any declaration on the part of Congress is nugatory; it is at least unnecessary.

The affair of the Barbary pirates was not one of the more important military conflicts in which the United States has been involved, but the incident does raise the fundamental constitutional questions presented by the specific manner in which the war powers are distributed in a very pointed and practical way. Clearly, reason and common sense are on the side of Hamilton's view that the open and avowed initiation of hostilities by a foreign nation against the United States creates a state of war just as certainly as if Congress had made a formal declaration, and the President has the full panoply of his powers as Commander in Chief to fight the war no less reservedly in the one case than in the other.

Hamilton's construction, valid enough in the case of the Barbary pirates, is even more relevant today. There is no reason to think that if the Kremlin should decide to make war upon the United States it will give us any more warning than did the Japanese at Pearl Harbor. Hamilton's logic is equally applicable to an attack, declared or undeclared, against the United States or against any of its armed forces, territories, or installations anywhere in the world. It is not difficult to conceive of a situation in which an attack upon the American zone in West Berlin might be due to the rashness, misunderstanding, or even intoxication of a Russian army officer rather than to the real intention of the Soviet Union to make war on the United States. Indeed, in the present "balance of terror," it is not very likely that war would be started with an all-out atomic attack on the United States. But a localized attack, or the use of force to eject American troops from Berlin or to cut off their communications, could very well be based upon the calculation that the United States would not go to war with the Soviet Union in the defense of Berlin and might therefore yield to Russian arms. The President should be recognized to have the power to meet limited warfare with limited warfare, or massive attack with massive retaliation.

The case of an atomic attack against the continental United States raises even more complicated questions, but Hamilton's thesis seems still to be valid. In the event our DEW-line screen indicated that Russian bombers, or Russian ballistic missiles, were headed toward the United States, would a presidential order for a counterattack be constitutional on the ground that the launching of the bombers or missiles constituted an act of war? If the American warning system were in error, and the Russians had merely launched another astronaut, or if the missile carried no warhead and was directed to the South Atlantic, the mistake would produce a holocaust of truly cosmic proportions. With the hazard so great and the time so short, we could only trust to the President's judgment and pray that his decision were the right one.

THE PRESIDENT AND INTERNAL SECURITY

The duties and responsibilities of the President with respect to foreign relations and military affairs stand, as shown, upon a special footing. This is due in part to the way in which the Constitution distributes between the President and Congress these essentially executive functions. But it is due in even larger part to the fact that the United States is a sovereign state, living in a world of sovereign states, that the conditions to which our diplomacy and military force must respond are never within the exclusive control of the United States, and are sometimes not even susceptible to significant influence by the United States.

The duties and responsibilities of the President with respect to internal security are based upon quite different foundations. One of the important cases illustrating the nature of the President's role in internal security grew out of the Pullman strike in 1894. Following a 25 per cent wage reduction in its shops by the Pullman Company, the shop employees, who were organized as a local of the American Railway Union, went on strike. The American Railway Union forbade its members to service Pullman cars after the Pullman Company refused to arbitrate. The interruption of rail service which resulted from the carrying into effect of the resolution of the American Railway Union created serious obstacles to the movement of interstate commerce and the delivery of the mails. Although the paralysis of services centered in Chicago, it quickly spread to other areas and other states. President Cleveland ordered the Attorney General to petition the Federal circuit court for a sweeping injunction against the members of the American Railway Union, which was granted and the constitutionality of which was subsequently sustained by the Supreme Court in *In re Debs*.

The injunction went unheeded, violence increased, and the United States marshal in Chicago reported that he was unable to carry out the orders of the Court. President Cleveland thereupon sent Federal troops to Chicago. The President's action was taken without consulting the authorities of the state of Illinois, and Governor Altgeld protested the sending of the troops, requesting their immediate withdrawal from active duty in the state. President Cleveland[11] replied to Governor Altgeld in the following words:

> Federal troops were sent to Chicago in strict accordance with the Constitution and laws of the United States, upon the demand of the Post-Office Department that obstruction of the mails should be removed, and upon the representation of the judicial officers of the United States that process of the federal courts could not be executed through the ordinary means, and upon abundant proof that conspiracies existed against commerce between the States. To meet these conditions, which are clearly within the province of Federal authority, the presence of Federal troops in the city of Chicago was deemed not only proper but necessary; and there has been no intention of thereby interfering with the plain duty of the local authorities to preserve the peace of the city.

A basic principle of Anglo-American jurisprudence is that normally compulsion is a derivative of judicial procedure. Military force is invoked, therefore, only when the ordinary civil enforcement of judicial decisions is impossible. Clearly, it is the judgment of the President that determines whether ordinary civil enforcement is possible. But is a

[11] Grover Cleveland, *Presidential Problems*, Century Company, New York, 1904, p. 111.

judicial determination, i.e., the injunction in the Pullman strike, a necessary precedent to constitutional action by the President in using military force? *In re Debs* seems to support the position advanced in Cleveland's telegram to Altgeld—that the President had power to act directly to assure the enforcement of the laws, with or without prior judicial determination. The decision[12] reads, in part, as follows:

> The strong arm of the national government may be put forth to brush away all obstructions to the freedom of interstate commerce or the transportation of the mails. If the emergency arises, the army of the Nation, and all of its militia, are at the service of the Nation to compel obedience to its laws. . . .

Cleveland was severely criticized for his action in the Pullman strike. Rich points out that while some action by the United States government was probably essential, Cleveland appears to have acted without much investigation.[13] It is true that he made no attempt to mediate the labor dispute, but acted simply to break the strike. It is likewise true that while he had no constitutional obligation to consult with the authorities of the state of Illinois and the city of Chicago, or even to notify them of his proposed action, this omission was from almost every other point of view arrogant and inexcusable. But this was the day of the "yellow dog" contract, company police, and the sweeping labor injunction. Perhaps the best—and the worst—thing that can be said of Cleveland's action in this instance is that he faithfully reflected the mores of his time.

Review Questions

1. What is the essential problem of the President in the exercise of his functions as Chief Executive?

2. What are the three principal powers that sustain the President's role as Chief Executive?

3. What is meant by administrative management?

4. What is involved in the President's performance of his duties as chief administrator?

[12] 158 U.S. 564 (1894).
[13] Bennett Milton Rich, *The Presidents and Civil Disorder*, The Brookings Institution, Washington, 1941, pp. 91–109.

5. What are the important staff agencies assisting the President in the overall management of the government?

6. What is the only-channel doctrine?

7. What are the major strengths and weaknesses of the President in the handling of foreign relations?

8. What does the Constitution mean in designating the President as Commander in Chief?

9. What are the principal limitations upon presidential discretion in the performance of his functions as Commander in Chief?

10. Why are the powers of the President with respect to internal order and security so much narrower than those relating to foreign affairs?

11. In what specific aspects did President Cleveland's actions in the Pullman strike illustrate the difference between presidential authority in internal affairs and foreign relations?

12. In what respects was Cleveland's action in the Pullman strike similar to Eisenhower's action in the Little Rock school crisis? In what respect was it different? What produced the difference?

THE PRESIDENT AND CONGRESS

Chapter 3

PRESIDENTIALISM AND CONGRESSIONALISM

The phrases "congressional government" and "the presidential system" are sometimes used loosely to mean about the same thing. The purposes of this analysis, however, clearly require a more precise definition. Congressionalism may be regarded as that state or condition of government in which the influence of the legislature is generally predominant, and presidentialism as that state or condition in which the executive provides the major influence and leadership. The dichotomy is by no means absolute, and even in periods in which the President is obviously in overall command, the Congress may lead on certain issues of public policy. Moreover, in recent times the Court, not ordinarily a source of policy leadership, has been the moving force on two major issues—desegregation of the public schools and the redistricting of national and state legislatures so as to achieve the equal value of the suffrage.

The ceaseless struggle for power between the President and the Congress is implicit in a constitutional system in which authority is so intricately distributed and in which interdependence is so pervasive. If, as it is alleged, nature abhors a vacuum, it is equally true that politics abhors an equilibrium. Two great energy systems, each with powers of aggression and defense, each active in areas which vitally involve the interests of the other, and neither able to operate without some degree of concurrence from the other unavoidably become involved in a contest as to which shall receive the superior accommodation at any particular time. When to the sources of conflict instinct in the structure of the government are added those which derive from the political system that has grown up around the Constitution a normally adversary relationship between the President and the Congress is well-nigh inevitable.

The immediate sources of conflict may be identified as: (1) legislative versus executive interests, (2) local versus national interests, (3) special versus general interests, (4) Democratic versus Republican interests. These sources of conflict are readily identifiable in the discussions which take place in either house of Congress when important legislation is under consideration. They are even more dramatically apparent in legislative consideration of administration measures. One of the classic cases in which the adversary relationships were played out with the inevitability of a Greek tragedy was the Senate Committee on Banking and Currency consideration in 1946 of the administration's bill for extending price control into the postwar period.[1]

The President was convinced that World War I experience supported the extension of price control. Starting in 1914 prices increased steadily until certain voluntary controls checked the rise in 1917–1918. Immediately after the Armistice in 1918 there was a slight recession, but by 1919–1920 prices had resumed their upward spiral, causing a great expansion of demand on the one hand and a hoarding of inventories in anticipation of even higher prices on the other. A buyers' strike then produced a collapse of the price structure followed by deflation and a sharp depression. During World War II price controls and rationing

[1] Ralph K. Huitt, "The Roles of Congressional Committee Members," *American Political Science Review*, 1954, vol. 48, pp. 340–365.

had kept the economy on a reasonably steady keel. The President was afraid that the precipitate relaxation of controls at the end of the war would lead to the repetition of the events which followed World War I.

The conflict between legislative and executive interests is perhaps best exemplified in the committee's discussion of the administrative record of the Office of Price Administration and its motives. The President's men were charged with dilatory tactics in handling appeals, with issuing incomprehensible regulations, and with tying up business with red tape. They were accused of continuously and directly disregarding the Price Control Act. One antiadministration witness testified that "For four years the OPA has thumbed its nose at Congress, has violated the basic law under which it was created, and has pursued an illegal but politically expedient course which has fed the fires of inflation and then tried to control the fire by stopping up the chimney." They were sharply criticized for allegedly refusing to grant relief in hardship cases, which they were empowered to do by law, and of impeding production by maintaining inadequate ceiling prices which they were authorized to raise. The antiadministration group thought the President's men in the OPA were theoretical economists, unversed in business, attempting to instruct experienced business men in their own affairs.

The performance of Senator Bankhead of Alabama was a simon-pure portrayal of the conflict between the local or sectional interest and the national interest. Bankhead was against price control for one reason and one reason only. He regarded it as inimical to the interests of his constituency in Alabama. He was interested in Southern cotton farmers and the textile industry to which they sell their product. His questioning of witnesses revealed this preoccupation at every turn. The testimony of a lumber industry witness was turned into a discussion of timber on land owned by farmers, and the price of southern as compared with western pine. Evidence on OPA profit calculation formulas became an attack by Bankhead on its methods of figuring profits in the textile industry.

The conflict between special interests and the general interest in the consideration of the price control bill was exemplified in two ways—first, the obvious involvement of individual senators with specific businesses and industries; and second, the way in which senators reacted to the testimony of representatives of major interest groups appearing before the committee. Capehart took up a good deal of the committee's time asking OPA officials about the trouser problem, concerning which he had received three telegrams from trouser vendors who alleged mistreatment at the hands of the OPA. Taylor was interested in the plaint of a packer in Idaho, and Mitchell in that of a packing plant in Tacoma. In some of the cases in which senators intervened in behalf of specific businesses and industries they were performing no more than the messenger-boy functions which constituents traditionally exact from their elected representatives. But in most instances they were responding to the steady, persistent, and tremendously powerful pressure that special economic interests are able to exert at the grass roots on members of the Senate and House of Representatives.

The legislation on the extension of price control provided in a very real sense the occasion for a testing of strength between large and powerful organized interest groups. The National Association of Manufacturers was against the extension of price control, for reasons which had nothing to do with the general interest and everything to do with the welfare of the economic interests represented by the association. The Congress of Industrial Organizations and the American Federation of Labor were for the extension of price control, likewise for reasons that were not primarily connected with the general interest but of great importance to the labor constituency. While the issue was basically between labor and management groups, another special interest organization, the American Farm Bureau Federation, intervened on the question of farm prices.

The debate, which involved basically how the various special interests had fared and expected to fare in the postwar economy, was extremely complicated. It involved the causes of inflation, the overall effect of price control, and the situation of labor and the farmers. There was bitter controversy on whether price control in fact controlled. There was fundamentally conflicting evidence on whether farm prices and industrial wages were up or down.

The antiadministration group, backed up by the NAM, thought that the OPA itself was the chief threat to the economy, and a major cause of inflation. OPA had followed a policy of keeping prices artificially low, as a result of which producers had been compelled to concentrate on their high-priced lines or introduce inferior substitutes. OPA's refusal to recognize increasing production costs in its pricing policies had retarded reconversion and civilian production. Its propaganda about hoarding and the need for price control, moreover, was primarily responsible for inflation psychology and panic purchasing.

The question of farm prices and industrial wages was a touchy one. With respect to industrial wages, the antiadministration group made much over the fact that hourly wage rates were up, but they refused to consider the fact that aggregate take-home pay was down. Hourly

wages are, of course, a part of the cost of production, and affect the
rate at which the producer can sell his goods. He naturally looks at
wages in terms of hourly rates. But the worker looks at his take-home
pay, since that is what he must use to pay the rent and buy the gro-
ceries. Senator Taft had refused to deal with anything except straight-
time hourly earnings since before the war. Green of the AFL was much
more interested in the decline of earnings since V-E Day. This hiatus
was never bridged.

To Senator Taft the contest over the extension of price controls was
just another round in the continuing battle between the Republicans
and the Democrats. He was against price controls, he was against the
British loan, and he was for the repeal of the excess profits tax because
they were the measures of a Democratic administration and *ipso facto*
bad. The fact that Taft was already running for the Republican presidential nomination in 1948 undoubtedly contributed to his essentially
partisan approach. He made it quite clear that it was the Democrats
he was fighting in his reply to Chester Bowles who protested at one
point that Taft was attributing to him views which he did not hold.
Taft said:

> Mr. Bowles, may I say this: I don't distinguish you
> from the Administration. The Administration has
> one policy; you are the Director of Economic Sta-
> bilization. What your particular views are make no
> difference to me. You are carrying on the policies
> of the Administration. When I say "You" I should
> be more explicit. I mean the Administration. I am
> not attacking you personally on it, or anything of
> the sort. I am criticizing your analysis of the situa-
> tion which is only affected by Administration pol-
> icy; not by what you personally think. That makes
> no difference to me.

THE IMPERATIVES OF PRESIDENTIAL LEADERSHIP

Woodrow Wilson[2] summed up the case for presidential leadership in
legislation in these words:

> Leadership in government naturally belongs to its
> executive officers, who are daily in contact with

[2] Woodrow Wilson, *Constitutional Government in the United States*, Columbia University Press, New York, 1961, pp. 72–73.

practical exigencies and whose reputations alike for good judgment and for fidelity are at stake much more than are those of the members of the legislative body at every turn of the law's application. The law-making part of the government ought certainly to be very hospitable to the suggestions of the planning and acting part of it. . . . Some of our Presidents have felt the need, which unquestionably exists in our system for some spokesman of the nation as a whole, in matters of legislation no less than in other matters, and have tried to supply Congress with the leadership of suggestion, backed by argument and by iteration and by every legitimate appeal to public opinion.

In early 1941, almost a year before Pearl Harbor, it was evident that the wage-price spiral was beginning to exert a deleterious effect upon the nation's transition from a peacetime to a wartime economy. That some steps would have to be taken by the government was clear, but upon the order of the steps to be taken the President and Congress were in sharp disagreement. In its simplest form, the President wanted to begin with price control, and subsequently to superimpose wage control when wages had risen to the point that assured labor of a viable standard of living. Congress, on the other hand, was more sensitive to the farm vote; it wanted wage control and then price control, and inserted in the Price Control Act of January 30, 1942, a provision that ceilings on food products should not become operative until farm prices had reached 110 per cent of parity.

By early 1942 the price-wage spiral had come to be a matter of the gravest concern to the President and his advisers. By April, the President had apparently decided to break the stalemate with Congress by agreeing to stabilize wages and prices at the same time. On April 27 he laid before Congress a seven-point economic program, of which two points required legislation—tax revision and permission to fix ceilings on farm products at parity prices.

Congress continued to dally. On September 7 the President cracked the whip with one of the strongest messages in the history of presidential-congressional relations.[3]

---

[3] *The Public Papers and Addresses of Franklin D. Roosevelt 1942*, pp. 364–365.

We cannot hold the actual cost of food and clothing down to approximately the present level beyond October first. But no one can give any assurances that the cost of living can be held down after that date.

Therefore, I ask the Congress to pass legislation under which the President would be specifically authorized to stabilize the cost of living, including the prices of all farm commodities. The purpose should be to hold farm prices at parity, or at levels of a recent date, whichever is higher.

I ask the Congress to take this action by the first of October. Inaction on your part by that date will leave me with an inescapable responsibility to the people of this country to see to it that the war effort is no longer imperiled by threat of economic chaos.

In the event that the Congress should fail to act, and act adequately, I shall accept the responsibility, and I will act.

At the same time that farm prices are stabilized, wages can and will be stabilized also. This I will do.

The President's message asked Congress to act upon the seven-point program which he had laid before it in April. He gave Congress an ultimatum, in effect, by setting a deadline—October 1. In the absence of appropriate action by the deadline, he announced that he would issue Executive orders to achieve his purposes. There was an inference that if he were forced to act by Executive order, the matter would be discussed fully with the country and might become an issue in the next election. Indeed, the President went on the air for a 30-minute "fireside chat" the evening of the same day the message was sent to Congress, and in his address to the people the President pointed out Congress' duty in quite specific and unmistakable terms. Congress apparently got the message, and almost by the prescribed deadline the requested price control act was on the President's desk for signature.

CONSTITUTIONAL POWERS OF LEADERSHIP

The Constitution confers powers of legislative leadership upon the President in only four matters—the recommendation of measures to the Congress, the calling of special sessions, the adjournment of Congress in certain circumstances, and the veto of measures passed by the Congress. Article II, section 3, provides:

> He shall from time to time give to the Congress Information of the State of the Union, and recommend to their Consideration such Measures as he shall judge necessary and expedient; he may, on extraordinary Occasions, convene both Houses, or either of them, and in Case of Disagreement between them, with Respect to the Time of Adjournment, he may adjourn them to such Time as he shall think proper. . . .

Article I, section 7, paragraphs 2 and 3, provides for the veto:

> Every Bill which shall have passed the House of Representatives and the Senate shall, before it becomes a Law, be presented to the President of the United States; If he approves he shall sign it, but if not he shall return it, with his Objections to that House in which it shall have originated, who shall enter the Objections at large on their Journal, and proceed to reconsider it. If after such Reconsideration two thirds of that House shall agree to pass the Bill, it shall be sent, together with the Objections, to the other House, by which it shall likewise be reconsidered, and if approved by two thirds of that House, it shall become a Law.

Messages from the President on the State of the Union have been presented to Congress since Washington's first term. The Constitution, in fact, makes this a duty. And Presidents have influenced legislation from the beginning—none more pervasively than Thomas Jefferson. But the emergence of the constitutional power of recommendation as an important device of legislative leadership is a modern development that dates from the Presidency of Theodore Roosevelt. The contribution of Theodore Roosevelt to the presidential message was two-fold: first, he used the address on the State of the Union to present his legislative demands to the Congress with a vigor and insistency new to the traditions of presidential communication; second, and much more important, he brought into public view and legitimized the practice of sending bills from the White House to the Capitol as avowed administration measures.

It remained for Woodrow Wilson to provide another important innovation in the use of the power of recommendation. Theodore Roosevelt and Taft had continued the tradition of sending an omnibus State of the Union message to Congress, with legislative proposals sandwiched into the enormous compilation of second-hand prose salvaged from departmental reports. The inevitable operation of a sort of Gresham's law of communication tended to obscure the pertinency of the President's legislative recommendations. Wilson, however, dramatized an important element in his legislative program by appearing before a special session of Congress to demand the passage of a new currency reform program. The result was the Federal Reserve Act, drafted largely in conferences at the White House, which the President then caused to be ratified by the Democratic caucus and hence made an obligatory party measure. It was enacted into law before the end of the year.

The constitutional message power of the President is, of course, basic. But it is only the beginning. Herman Finer,[4] writing primarily of the congressional leadership exercised by Theodore Roosevelt, Taft, and Wilson, described the processes in these words:

> They sent messages to the Houses, and letters to party friends; held conferences and breakfasts in their rooms adjoining the Senate, and invited the Chairmen of Committees and the "floor leaders" to the White House. Their most trusted and astute Cabinet officers were often sent to the Congressional lobbies to whip up support, and to exert the influence of personal representation of the President. Heads of departments attended caucus meetings; information was poured into Congress; party friends were provided with drafts of bills and the vindicating briefs.

All this was long before radio and television came to the support of presidential leadership. Nowadays the President can almost at will replenish his reserves of popular support with a fireside chat or a televised press conference beamed directly into the American home—the very source of the *vox populi* which to congressmen tends also to be the *vox Dei*.

The actual use of the veto as a negation of legislative action has

[4] Herman Finer, *Theory and Practice of Modern Government*, The Dial Press, Inc., New York, 1932, vol. II, p. 1034.

increased enormously throughout the course of American constitutional history. Its use as an instrument for bargaining with Congress has increased concomitantly. Indeed, the veto power was given to the President primarily so that he might defend himself against congressional encroachment on executive powers rather than to prevent the enactment of bad laws. Washington vetoed only two measures during his eight years in office, one because he thought the bill unconstitutional, and the other because he disapproved of the policy the bill embodied. Neither Adams nor Jefferson used the veto at all, but in Jefferson's two terms almost all bills that secured congressional approval were administration measures. Madison vetoed six bills, four on constitutional grounds and two on objections of policy. From the time of Jackson the use of the veto for reasons of policy and expediency became much more frequent, and constitutional arguments in veto messages have all but disappeared.

From Washington through Eisenhower the veto power was invoked 2,192 times. Of these 1,261 were messaged vetoes—i.e., bills returned by the President to the house of their origin with statements of his objections, and 931 were pocket vetoes—bills presented to the President within 10 days of the close of a session of Congress which died as result of his failure to sign them. Cleveland, Franklin D. Roosevelt, and Truman accounted for 68 per cent of the total vetoes since the beginning, 71 per cent of the messaged vetoes, and 61 per cent of pocket vetoes. Franklin D. Roosevelt, who established a number of records during his term of office, vetoed a larger proportion of bills sent him by Congress than any other President—he stopped approximately one in every twelve.[5] In general, the stronger the President the more frequently he makes use of his veto power.

The mere existence of the possibility of a presidential veto is sufficient normally to produce reasonably careful consultation of the President's views on the form and substance of pending legislation, including amendments to administration measures. But negative powers sometimes have positive implications. The President is able to say, in effect, to sponsors of legislative measures, "You want Bill A. I want Bill B. My attitude toward Bill A when it comes before me for signature or veto will be determined largely by your success in securing the passage of Bill B. Take care, therefore, that you send me Bill B in the proper form

[5] Franklin D. Roosevelt is alleged occasionally to have asked his staff for "something I can veto," just to serve as a reminder to Congress. See Richard Neustadt, *Presidential Power*, John Wiley & Sons, Inc., New York, 1960, p. 84.

and at the time when my discretion with respect to the signature of Bill A can be effectively exercised." Within this context it is clear that the veto is an important element in the President's arsenal of devices for the generation of the pressures essential to the achievement of his legislative purposes. As Richard Neustadt[6] puts it:

> With hardly an exception, the men who share in governing this country are aware that at some time, in some degree, the doing of *their* jobs, the furthering of *their* ambitions, may depend upon the President of the United States. Their need for presidential action, or their fear of it, is bound to be recurrent if not actually continuous. Their need or fear is his advantage.

POLITICAL POWERS OF LEADERSHIP

The President's constitutional powers of leadership are important, but they are important primarily because they facilitate and sustain the exercise of his political powers of leadership. The President may send a message to Congress, but the significance of his message depends upon what Congress then does. He may call a special session, but his summons will be notable only if the special session achieves notable results. He may veto a bill, or threaten a veto, but whether he makes history is determined by his success in pushing through his legislative program, not by the fate of a few random congressional enactments. In short, the acid test of presidential leadership of Congress lies in his political achievements, to which his constitutional powers of leadership are ancillary.

Where do his political powers of leadership come from? They come from a wholly extraconstitutional development which the framers never contemplated. The movement in concert of the separate branches of government, especially the executive and legislative organs, has been produced by the operation of forces wholly external to the Constitution itself. The party system, however poor the harmony and however ragged the concert it achieves, does redistribute the powers divided in the Constitution, and reassembles them in a shifting and kaleidoscopic pattern which permits the government to move, and sometimes permits it to move with remarkable agility. Bellquist tells us:[7]

[6] *Ibid.*, p. 35.
[7] "Congressionalism and Parliamentarism," in John C. Wahlke and Heinz Eulau (eds.), *Legislative Behavior*, The Free Press of Glencoe, New York, 1959, pp. 40–41.

The party system is the unwritten constitution which helps to make the written constitution work, which brings the ends of Pennsylvania Avenue together. Only from this point of view can its illogicalities be explained, and its strength be appreciated. Moreover, political practice has shown that the influence actually exerted by a department of the government depends not so much upon the legal authority which it enjoys in law or theory as upon the great interests which function through it in reality. The people holding office and the time during which office is held greatly determine the amount of power exercised.

The President is the head of his party. He is also the political leader of the nation. By rubbing these two sticks together a determined President is able to kindle many a fire. Woodrow Wilson[8] summed it up in these words:

[The President] cannot escape being the leader of his party except by incapacity and lack of personal force, because he is at once the choice of the party and the nation. He is the party nominee, and the only party nominee for whom the whole nation votes. Members of the House and Senate are representatives of localities, are voted for only by sections of voters. . . . There is no national party choice except that of President. No one else represents the people as a whole exercising a national choice; and inasmuch as his strictly executive duties are subordinated, so far at any rate as all detail is concerned, the President represents not so much the party's governing efficiency as its ideals and principles. He is not so much part of its organization as its vital link of connection with the thinking nation. He can dominate his party by being spokesman for the real sentiment and purpose of the country, by giving direction to opinion, by giving the country at once the information and the statements of policy which will enable it to form its judgments alike of parties and of men. . . .

8 *Op. cit.*, p. 67.

The President is, in fact, party leader at one time, leader of national opinion at another, and sometimes simultaneously leader both of the party and national opinion. When this latter condition prevails, the President's power reaches its maximum, and the country experiences something like Franklin D. Roosevelt's Hundred Days. But such periods do not long prevail, and no matter how large his congressional majority the President normally operates in a politically adversary relationship with Congress in which his leadership derives from his ability to seize issues with strong public appeal and create pressures, both by appeal to the general opinion and by political manipulation on the Hill, which result in something approximating the desired congressional action.

Despite the President's enormous influence in both the initiation and control of legislation, his task of legislative leadership involves the most devastating kind of intellectual, physical, and spiritual travail. It involves compromise. Sometimes it even involves defeat. One of the most important programs of the New Deal was its attempt to protect the interests of wage earners, especially those who did not have the protection of labor unions in collective bargaining, through the establishment of national minimum wages and maximum hours. Franklin D. Roosevelt devoted twelve months of hard labor to preparing the way for the Fair Labor Standards Act of 1938, only to have it completely emasculated when it was introduced to a Congress that was 80 per cent Democratic, and had in the main ridden into office on the President's coattails.[9]

The lobbies of business and industry were, of course, expected to oppose the bill, and these expectations were not disappointed. It was anticipated that the labor unions, on the other hand, would support the legislation. This expectation was disappointed, because while both the Congress of Industrial Organizations and the American Federation of Labor were in favor of legislation on labor standards they could not agree on the version of the legislation they would support.

In the Senate committee, where the President's bill was originally introduced, the special interest groups were able to write into the bill so many exceptions and exemptions that its effectiveness was seriously impaired. Even in its emasculated condition, the bill narrowly escaped recommitment when it reached the floor of the Senate by a vote of 48 to 36. In the House the treatment of the legislation was even more ruthless. The Rules Committee was dominated by Southern Democrats intent upon preserving the sectional advantage which they thought to reside in the generally lower wage rates prevailing in the South. The

[9] Herman Finer, *The Presidency: Crisis and Regeneration*, The University of Chicago Press, Chicago, 1960, pp. 79–80.

Committee would not report a rule for the bill, and it even proved impossible to assemble a caucus of the Democrats in the House to get a party-line showdown for support of a motion to discharge the Committee and bring the bill to the floor. The bill was still in committee when Congress adjourned.

The President then called the Congress back into special session. This served to focus the attention of the country on the issue, and to emphasize the importance of the legislation the President delivered a series of radio addresses explaining the benefits the bill would confer. The continued recalcitrance of the southerners again compelled the President and his congressional supporters to fall back upon a discharge petition. After several months of intensive labor, involving the use of patronage, the trading of agricultural legislation for farm-bloc votes, and almost every other weapon in the President's political arsenal the 218 signatures necessary to bring the discharge petition to a vote were secured.

The AFL, apparently preferring to see no fair labor standards legislation enacted rather than a bill associated with the rival CIO, chose this moment to secure the introduction of an entirely new and different labor standards bill. The business and industrial lobbies, which were intent upon defeating any fair labor standards legislation if possible, launched a heavily financed campaign to alienate farm-bloc support by attempting to convince farmers that the legislation would increase their labor costs and raise the prices of manufactured goods. The Southern Democrats and the friends of the AFL in Congress were, for different reasons, equally intent upon defeating the CIO. One of the bills was killed, and by the time the other was reported it had been so thoroughly mutilated that it was worse than no bill at all.

But the President was determined that a fair labor standards act of some sort should be passed by the Seventy-fifth Congress. His original bill was recalled and sent to the Department of Labor for redrafting. He reopened negotiations with the American Federation of Labor, the farm bloc, the Southern Democrats, and other obstructionist elements. The House Labor Committee set one of its subcommittees which had not been involved in the previous bills to work looking for a new formula upon which agreement might be reached, without success. This Committee likewise was unable to report out any version of the President's bill, in consequence of which he shifted to the American Federation of Labor bill and was successful in having it rewritten to include some of the salient provisions of his own original proposal.

The bill was finally passed by the House in May. A conference committee then spent three weeks reconciling the House and Senate versions, and the bill was signed. The President had been successful in getting a fair labor standards act out of the Congress. But the act he finally secured was far short of the objectives with which he started. It would require 2 years under the 1938 act to raise the minimum hourly wage to 40 cents and to lower the maximum workweek to 44 hours. Under the discretionary provisions of the act exemptions would be sought and secured for many industries. The southerners had demanded and received their pound of flesh in the form of differential minima to meet regional conditions and preserve their favored position resulting from substandard wage scales. The American Federation of Labor had demanded and received a guarantee that in no case would minimum wage rates be set below prevailing levels, which further impaired the uniform application of the law; most of all it had dealt a telling blow to John L. Lewis and the Congress of Industrial Organizations.

PERSPECTIVES OF COOPERATION

The friction losses inherent in the adversary relationship between the President and Congress have been the cause of concern to both students and practitioners of American politics. They have been of concern to the partisans of presidential leadership as well as the partisans of congressional authority. To a considerable degree they are the price that must be paid for a system which seeks to safeguard liberty by dividing and sharing power and responsibility. Fundamentally the question turns on considerations of political and moral values, not of governmental mechanics. We must at least consider the hypothesis that friction and conflict have, in our system, their own positive virtues.

Since the alleged evil springs from different sources, the remedies that have been offered are devised to cure quite different things. Some seek to improve communication between the President and Congress, presumably on the principle that if the two ends of Pennsylvania Avenue understand each other fully the causes of conflict will disappear. As early as July, 1789, Secretary of Foreign Affairs Jay appeared before the Senate and gave it information concerning international matters pending in that body. As late as 1945 the then Rep. Estes Kefauver of Tennessee introduced a resolution to amend Rule XXIII of the House of Representatives to open the floor to heads of departments, agencies, and independent establishments, and to set up regular question periods during which they might be interrogated. In the years between many similar proposals have been advanced.

None has been adopted, primarily because they are all irrelevant. The real business of Congress is transacted in its committees; what takes place on the floor is normally the ratification, without significant change, of what has been decided in the committees. Heads of departments and agencies find it relatively easy to gain access to the committees and are able to state their cases at the places and times when their statements may have results. By the time an issue reaches the floor it is no longer an issue—it has been decided. On the other hand, when congressional committees are seeking information they can proceed much more expeditiously through the regular or special investigatory process than through so formalized and pretentious a process as a "question period" on the floor.

Somewhat more plausible are the proposals for a joint executive-legislative council which probably originated in a committee of the American Political Science Association, and were urged without success by George B. Galloway upon the La Follette–Monroney Committee which drafted the Legislative Reorganization Act of 1946. Presumably such a council would provide the forum in which a modus vivendi could be worked out in advance and during the course of legislative proceedings in such a manner as to minimize the overt friction which now characterizes relations between the President and Congress. On the other hand, the joint council assumes a measure of discipline in the congressional party which the facts rarely justify, and it also ignores the enormous differences in the constituency of the President's congressional majority from one important administration measure to another.

Even stronger proposals would substitute, in effect, a legislative cabinet for the existing presidential Cabinet, the advice of which the President would be obligated to seek in respect to matters presented by the administration to the Congress. This proposal is responsive to the generally recognized ineffectiveness of the Cabinet as presently constituted as a source of political counsel. But the likelihood of a constructive political advisory relationship between the President and a cabinet drawn from a group of senators and congressmen seconded on the seniority principle, which is the only way the houses have developed for constituting their leadership, is very dubious. It is, moreover, contrary to the facts of presidential power. The President's power comes from his relationship to the people. Adroitly employed, it is frequently sufficient to overcome the lethargy or even the outright opposition of members of Congress possessing neither the breadth of his constituency nor the quality of his intimacy with the sources of political power. To surrender his initiative and limit his goals to what he is able to persuade a "cabinet" of senior representatives of the two houses to approve is to defraud the legitimate expectations of the people. There is much more control than useful support in the proposal for a cabinet drawn from members of the Senate and House of Representatives. It calls upon the President to give up powers of initiative and leadership which he cannot surrender and remain the leader of the nation, and it gives to a cabal of Congress a control of the President for which it has no corresponding responsibility. Moreover, it gives to the President no support or assistance which he cannot secure at present by direct negotiation with his party leaders in the Congress.

Many American political scientists, over many decades, have been consistently intrigued—and misled—by the admirable characteristics of British parliamentary institutions, and have sought in various ways to graft cabinet government onto the presidential stem established by the Constitution. Some of these proposals return to the battle fought, and lost, in Philadelphia in 1787 by the proponents of a plural executive, and seek to replace the President with an executive board having collective responsibility and the power of dissolution of Congress. Others believe that friction losses would be eliminated if the President (by Executive order) and the Congress (by concurrent resolution) were authorized in the Constitution to dissolve the government and call for simultaneous elections of the President, the Senate, and the House. An important element of all these proposals is the injection into the arena of executive-legislative relationships of the sobering influence presumed to reside in the threat of dissolution and general election. But the obvious fact that electoral power in the United States is completely federalized, that national political parties are nothing more than loose alliances of state and local political organizations hastily cobbled together each four years for the purpose of attempting to capture the Presidency, and that there is no authority or influence in the national political party between national presidential elections except what the President gives it, mean that the party system provides no such substructure of nationally disciplined power as that required by the various sorts of parliamentary government that have been suggested. Dissolution poses no effective threat in American politics, because elections answer few questions with respect to the specifics of public policy.

In a different, but related, tradition is the call of the American Political Science Association's committee on political parties for the tightening of national party discipline.[10] This, presumably, would give the

[10] "Toward a More Responsible Two-Party System," *American Political Science Review, Supplement*, September, 1950.

President as the head of the national party a more effective instrument of presidential leadership in legislation and in national administration as well. None would deny that a compact, well-organized working majority in the houses, disciplined by the President's direction of the party rather than by the particularistic leadership of the chairmen of the standing committees in the two houses, would make the President's job much easier. But our political system provides no fulcrum by which discipline of this nature might be achieved. Party discipline is a function of the power of the party to determine the political future of an elected official. That power the National Committee, the congressional party, or even the President does not possess. They will never possess it so long as electoral power is organized and wielded on a state or even local basis. And the prospects for the nationalizing of electoral power are dim indeed.

Perhaps the best advice on the subject of presidential leadership and of the Presidency in general comes from Clinton Rossiter,[11] who tells us to "leave it alone." An able and determined President is not without resources for securing congressional compliance with measures for which he is able to generate public support. Congress is not without resources, whenever it chooses to assert its corporate authority and power, for containing a President in measures which it regards as unwise or as lacking in public support. The conflict and clash of interests in the hammering out of public policy and government action may well be the best guarantee both of the acceptability of the end and the suitability of the means. It is certainly the best guarantee of liberty, which is the supreme value of our entire social system and the acid test of our political arrangements.

Review Questions

1. From your knowledge of American history, draw up a table indicating the periods which, in your opinion, were characterized by "presidentialism" and those which were characterized by "congressionalism." What are your reasons?

2. What are the immediate sources of conflict between the President and Congress?

3. In what specific ways did the hearings of the Sen-

---

[11] Clinton Rossiter, *The American Presidency*, Harcourt, Brace & World, Inc., New York, 1960, pp. 258–262.

ate Commission on Banking and Currency on the extension of price controls in 1946 illustrate these sources of conflict?

      4. Why is presidential leadership of Congress important in the American government?

      5. What are the four constitutional powers of legislative leadership conferred upon the President, which are the more important, and how are the important constitutional powers exercised?

      6. What are the primary sources of the President's political powers of legislative leadership? How does the President exercise his political powers of leadership?

      7. Outline briefly the characteristics of the five major categories of proposals that have been made to lessen presidential-congressional friction. Why has none of them been adopted?

CONGRESS: FUNCTIONS AND ORGANIZATION

Chapter 4

Members of Congress are fond of referring to it as "the greatest legislative body on earth." Whether it is the greatest may be disputed, but Congress is undoubtedly the most powerful legislative body in the world. With the great expansion of the Federal government, which today has an annual budget of over $100 billion, and more than two and one half million employees, Congress passes upon policies and programs which affect the economy not only of this country but of the free world. Formerly members of Congress were concerned almost wholly with domestic issues and policies, but today there are few major bills before Congress which do not have an impact on international as well as national affairs.

At the end of World War II many informed persons doubted that the President and the Congress would be able to work effectively together in the determination of domestic and international policies that would be required in the postwar period. Many doubted that this country would be able to meet the challenge of providing international leadership that was thrust upon it. These doubters were keenly aware of the built-in conflict between the two branches of government, the perennial struggle between the President and Congress over foreign affairs, the absence of disciplined political parties, and the tendency of Congress to debate and delay but fail to act on urgent public policies.

The events since 1945 have not borne out these doubts and fears. The United States has been able to act on urgent international problems and to provide leadership of the free nations in international affairs. Despite occasional conflicts between the President and the Congress, and the fact that during most of the period since the end of the war the President has been opposed by a majority of Congress (including bipartisan coalitions), the two branches of government have shown a remarkable degree of cooperation in international affairs. Their differences have been more marked in domestic affairs, where the government has often been unable to cope with pressing problems. Congress has adjusted its organization and procedures to meet its new and vastly greater responsibilities, though further reforms are needed. Since 1946 Congress has improved its committee system, strengthened its staff and procedures, enormously increased its expenditures for investigations, and is far better equipped than formerly to act upon legislation and to watch over the administration.

FUNCTIONS AND POWERS

The most important function of Congress is that of passing laws. It shares the legislative power with the President, who recommends policies and legislation and can veto bills passed by Congress. A two-thirds majority of each house is then required to override the veto. The legislative power of Congress is granted by Article I of the Constitution, which provides that it shall have the powers, among others, to lay and collect taxes, to borrow money, to regulate commerce with foreign nations and among the states, to coin money and regulate the value thereof, to create inferior courts, to declare war, to raise and support an army and a navy, and "to make all laws which shall be necessary and proper for carrying into execution the foregoing powers, and all powers vested in the Government of the United States by this Constitution. . . ." Several of these powers are extremely broad. Under its power to levy taxes, for example, Congress was able to enact social security legislation which established a national system of old age, survivors', and disability insurance, a state system of unemployment compensation, and other welfare and health programs. Under its power over interstate commerce Congress is able to regulate wages, hours, conditions of work, and other aspects of management and labor relations, as well as to establish agricultural price support and crop control programs that were unknown until recent years.

Under its legislative power, Congress determines the programs that will be carried on by the government, establishes policies, and often prescribes procedures; regulates the armed forces; authorizes foreign-aid programs; fixes the duties on imports and controls our commerce with other countries; controls foreign policies; determines the broad policies for the regulation of transportation, communication, public power, trade practices, and the sale of securities; regulates the use of public lands; provides subsidies for large sectors of the economy; and does a thousand other things.

A second major function of Congress is control of the administration. It creates executive departments, authorizes their activities, fixes their objectives, and regulates their operations. Through the power to appropriate funds for the support of government Congress exercises one of its most potent controls over the executive departments. Before funds are voted, the appropriations committees review in considerable detail not only the department estimates, but their work plans, administration, and past performance. Many directions, both official and unofficial, are given to the departments by the appropriations committees. All standing legislative committees are directed by the Legislative Reorganization Act of 1946 to exercise continuous oversight of the departments within their purview.

A third function of Congress is to conduct investigations, not only of the administration of the executive departments, but into social and economic problems. Investigations are essential to provide Congress with the information and knowledge that it requires to legislate wisely on the multitude of public issues. Investigations are also used to inform the public, to build up public support for or opposition to government policies. They have often been used primarily to secure party or factional advantage, or to publicize an ambitious chairman. At times the investigative function has appeared to overshadow the other functions of Congress.

Another function of Congress is to educate and inform the public. Woodrow Wilson[1] wrote:

> It is the proper duty of a representative body to look diligently into every affair of government and to talk much about what it sees. It is meant to be the eyes and the voice, and to embody the wisdom and will of its constituents. . . . The informing function of Congress should be preferred even to its legislative function.

The same point of view was expressed by John Stuart Mill:[2]

> I know not how a representative assembly can more usefully employ itself than in talk, when the subject of talk is the great public interests of the country, and every sentence of it represents the opinion either of some important body of persons in the nation, or an individual in whom some such body have reposed their confidence.

The informing function is performed today largely through committee hearings on important legislative proposals and through congressional investigations. Debate on the floor of each house has become largely a lost art, especially in the House of Representatives, which places severe limitations on the time allotted for debate. Although the level of debate in the Senate is higher, it is the proceedings of the major committees rather than the floor debates that attract greatest attention.

Congress also performs a variety of other functions. It proposes amendments to the Constitution and determines the method by which the states pass upon such amendments. It meets in joint session every four years to count the electoral votes, and in the event that no candidate for President receives a majority, the House of Representatives elects a President from the highest three candidates, each state casting one vote. Each house is the judge of its own elections and the qualifications of its own members. Either house may refuse to seat persons

[1] Woodrow Wilson, *Congressional Government*, Houghton Mifflin Company, Boston, 1885, p. 303.
[2] *On Liberty and Representative Government*, Oxford University Press, Fair Lawn, N.J., 1948, p. 175.

on any grounds that it chooses. The House of Representatives once refused to seat Victor Berger, a Socialist elected from Milwaukee, who was promptly reelected by the voters of his district and was subsequently seated.

The House of Representatives has the power to impeach civil officers of the United States, including the President, who thereupon are tried by the Senate, acting as a judicial body. A two-thirds vote of the Senate is required to convict an officer on impeachment charges. Although the framers of the Constitution anticipated that this procedure would provide the means for removing officers who were guilty of misconduct or abuse of their trust, the power has seldom been used.

Each chamber has the power to discipline its own members, a power that has rarely been used. The most famous recent case was the vote of censure of the late Sen. Joseph McCarthy of Wisconsin for conduct unbecoming a member of the Senate. Each house can expel a member by a two-thirds vote, an action that has not been taken for many years. Each house may punish a private person for conduct which interferes with its work and for contempt (as failure to answer questions put to him by an investigating committee) by ordering the Sergeant at Arms to hold him in custody. Such punishment, however, is limited to the period that Congress is in session. When Congress adjourns a person so incarcerated must be released. Congress follows the practice today of turning over recalcitrant witnesses who are cited for contempt to the Justice Department for prosecution.

Congress admits new states to the Union. Each house determines its own rules, except those provided in the Constitution itself. The Senate alone is granted the power to advise and consent to treaties and to approve or disapprove presidential nominations to most offices, civil and military. The requirement that treaties must be approved by a two-thirds vote of the Senate has given it preeminence over the House in foreign affairs, though legislation and appropriations to implement such treaties require the approval of both houses.

Although the powers granted to Congress are great, they are not unlimited. Bills which it passes and joint resolutions having the effect of law require the signature of the President, unless they are passed by a two-thirds majority by both houses over the President's veto. Acts of Congress are also subject to review by the courts and may be overruled on the ground that they are not within the powers granted to the Federal government by the Constitution, or violate some constitutional provision. It is the Supreme Court which determines the meaning of provisions of the Constitution and whether statutes passed by Congress, as well as the actions of executive officers, are constitutional.

THE ADOPTION OF A BICAMERAL LEGISLATURE

The decision of the framers of the Constitution to establish a bicameral legislative body consisting of the House of Representatives and the Senate was one of the "great compromises" of the Convention. The smaller states, fearing that a single legislative body apportioned among the states on the basis of population would lead to its domination by a few of the larger states, were able to secure the creation of a second chamber in which each state, regardless of population, would have equal representation. The fears of the smaller states proved to be groundless; there has seldom, if ever, been a division in the House of Representatives in which the more populous states were aligned on one side against the smaller states. But the system of representation which gives all states equal representation in the Senate is firmly established in the Constitution and cannot be changed without the consent of every state.

The framers of the Constitution feared that the lower house, being directly elected by the people and responsive to their demands, would be moved by popular passions and act hastily, violating the rights of property owners and the well-to-do. It was thought that the Senate, being a smaller body and composed of older persons selected by the state legislatures, would provide a check on radical legislation passed by the lower house. For the first hundred years the Senate was, indeed, the more conservative body, and, being composed largely of men of wealth, was called the "millionaires' club." Since the adoption of the Seventeenth Amendment in 1913, which provided for popular election of senators, the Senate has often been more liberal than the House of Representatives.

THE HOUSE OF REPRESENTATIVES

REAPPORTIONMENT Seats in the House of Representatives are apportioned among the several states on the basis of population as determined by the census every 10 years. Until 1930 it had been a common practice of Congress to increase the size of the House of Representatives after every census so that no state would lose seats, but in 1929 it passed an act which fixed by law the permanent number of House members at 435, and provided that after each decennial census the President shall report to Congress the population of each state and the number of seats to which it is entitled. Unless Congress acts to the contrary within 60 days thereafter, each state is allocated the number of seats thus indicated. States with the largest increases in population during the preceding decade receive additional seats at the expense of other states whose populations have not increased as rapidly as the nation. California, for example, whose population increased from 10,586,223 in 1950 to 15,717,304 in 1960, received eight additional seats in 1961, while a number of other states lost seats.

The congressional districts in each state are determined by the state legislature. The party in control of the state legislature customarily draws the district lines in a manner that enables it to elect a maximum number of representatives to Congress, and in so doing often draws districts of weird shapes and frequently of very unequal population. Formerly Federal apportionment acts required the state legislatures to establish districts of substantially equal population and of "compact and contiguous" territory, but these requirements had little effect, for until 1962 the courts held that reapportionment was a political decision and hence not reviewable in courts of law. In 1962 the United States Supreme Court reversed earlier rulings and held in the case of *Baker v. Carr* that a state apportionment could be set aside by Federal courts if it denied persons "equal protection of the laws," guaranteed by the Fourteenth Amendment. The case arose in Tennessee, where for 61 years the rural-controlled state legislature, despite great shifts in the population, had refused to redistrict the state. This historic ruling makes legislative apportionment acts subject to judicial review if they are grossly disproportionate to population.

Redistricting for partisan advantage is commonly known as "gerrymandering." Under Elbridge Gerry, an early governor of Massachusetts, the Legislature drew one congressional district of such grotesque shape that it was said to resemble a salamander, but was dubbed instead a "Gerrymander." The name has come to be applied to various methods used by legislatures in carving out districts of curious shapes and unequal populations for partisan advantage. The district lines are so drawn that a maximum number of districts will be safely carried by the party in power, with comfortable but not too large majorities, while the districts which are conceded to the opposition are not only large in population, but an attempt is made to concentrate as many opposition voters as possible within a single district. Incumbents of the party in control of the state legislature are given safe districts

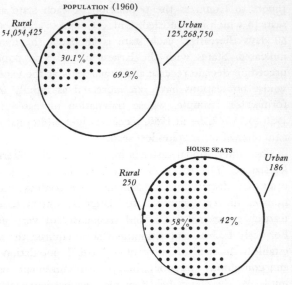

POPULATION (1960)

Rural
54,054,425

Urban
125,268,750

30.1%

69.9%

HOUSE SEATS

Urban
186

Rural
250

58% 42%

(At-large seat of Connecticut excluded)

Urban-rural representation in the House of Representatives. (Adapted from The New York Times, *February 4, 1962, p. E 10.)*

which assure their reelection, while incumbents of the opposite party may be forced to run in substantially new districts. Rural areas, which are almost invariably overrepresented in the state legislature, are often given seats in Congress out of proportion to their population (see figure). In addition, many congressmen from "safe" rural districts are reelected year after year, acquiring seniority and eventually the chairmanships of powerful standing committees. As a result, rural America has a disproportionate voice in the House of Representatives.

In contrast to the practice in the United States, the districts for the election of members of the House of Commons are determined by nonpartisan boundary commissions under standards established by Parliament. The states of Missouri and Florida have adopted constitutional amendments that similarly assign the task of redistricting to bipartisan bodies outside of the Legislature. It would appear that the only cure for gerrymandering is to assign the task of redistricting to a nonpartisan or bipartisan body.

ELECTION OF MEMBERS   Members of the House of Representatives are elected every two years. Hardly has the congressman arrived in Washington to take up his duties as a legislator before he must begin his campaign for reelection. The cost of primary and election campaigns is very high, especially in urban districts where the two parties are fairly evenly divided. In close contests it is not unusual for the campaign expenditures on behalf of the winning candidate to exceed $50,000, or more than his entire salary during his term of office. Of course, the candidate does not personally pay the entire cost of the campaign, though he often contributes a substantial amount. The high cost of campaigning is one of the least attractive features of American politics, for it places public officers under heavy obligations to the party organizations and to large contributors.

The nomination of candidates for Congress is strictly local. The national and state party organizations usually have nothing to do with it. The nominee is ordinarily chosen by the local party leaders and the party organization, to whom he feels heavily obligated. It is for this reason that members of Congress are more influenced by the wishes of local party leaders and their principal financial contributors than by national party leaders.

THE ROLE OF THE LEGISLATOR   Should a member of Congress be guided by the wishes of his constituents or should he act in the national interest on the basis of his judgment and study of the issues? As a representative, should he reflect the opinion and desires of his constituents, or should he exercise his own best judgment? This issue has long been debated by philosophers and legislators. In an address to the electors of the city of Bristol nearly two hundred years ago, Edmund Burke maintained that while it is the duty of a member of Parliament to keep in touch with his constituents and to look after their needs, he is elected by them to exercise "his unbiased opinion, his mature judgment, his enlightened conscience," and that to act contrary to his judgment is to betray those who elected him.

The first consideration of most members of Congress is to act in a manner that will ensure their reelection. Only by reelection over a period of years will they rise through seniority to positions of power and influence. Consequently, they are ordinarily most solicitous to serve the interests of their own districts, which are almost invariably put above the more uncertain national interest. Most members of Congress profess to be guided by the wishes of their constituents, and only a few assert a higher duty to act in the national interest, exercising their own judgment. On most issues that congressmen are called upon to vote there is little or no public opinion back home, and they must necessarily vote on the basis of their own judgment. On controversial and highly publicized issues they often receive letters and telegrams from constituents, but congressmen have learned that such representations are often inspired by an organized group and may not reflect the general opinion in their districts. Some members conduct opinion polls on leading issues by mailing questionnaires to constituents, but these are often slanted to elicit the answer desired by the congressmen. Consequently, on the great majority of issues the member of Congress must decide on the basis of his own judgment, but the interest of his own district, or of dominant elements in his district, is usually uppermost in his decision.

Members of Congress are usually able to reconcile both points of view. If they would be reelected they must vote in accord with the wishes of strong and well-organized groups in their districts, or at least in a manner that will not unnecessarily offend such groups. Congressmen, as a rule, support projects and programs of benefit to influential groups of voters in their districts, though they may have doubts about the wisdom of the national policy.

In order to build up support back home, members of Congress devote a large amount of their time and energy to rendering a variety of services to their constituents. If a citizen wants some action from a department such as a government contract, a son discharged from the armed services, a government job not under civil service, or if a veteran wants to appeal a decision affecting his pension and is unable to get the desired action from the department, he turns to his congressman for assistance. In many instances his request is merely for information and assistance in presenting his case to the proper authorities, but not infrequently the constituent is seeking special treatment or favors to which he is not entitled, and wants the congressman to put pressure on the department in his behalf. This activity is commonly called "running errands" for constituents, but obviously it involves a good deal more than errands. It takes a lot of the time of the Congressman and his staff, but it is a service that he must perform if he wants to be reelected. Some congressmen are scrupulous to avoid putting pressure on departments in behalf of constituents who want special favors to which they are not entitled; others are not so particular. Each member is given an allowance to maintain an office in his own district, to which voters are invited to bring their complaints and requests.

Congressmen, with the aid of local chambers of commerce and other local organizations, spend a large part of their time seeking Federal expenditures of benefit to their districts. Rivers and harbors that carry little traffic have been improved at large expense by the Federal government because of the influence of local congressmen, who team up with other members of Congress who have similar projects in their districts. Appropriations for local projects are "logrolled" through Congress, each member voting for the projects of other members in return for their support of his own. The voting of Federal appropriations for uneconomic projects has come to be called "pork," and the omnibus bill that includes projects for many districts is commonly labeled the "pork barrel." Military installations, hospitals, and other Federal facilities are often located in the districts of the Congressmen or Senators with the greatest political influence rather than at the best location. Despite the desire by many members of Congress for greater economy in government, they are forced to play the game and go after increased expenditures of benefit to their constituents.

THE PERSONNEL OF THE HOUSE   About 60 per cent of the members of both Houses of Congress are attorneys. The reasons are obvious. A large proportion of persons who enter the legal profession are interested in politics and become candidates for public office when the occasion presents itself. Attorneys who are members of law firms are better able to combine public office with a professional career than are persons in other occupations, and often profit by the added law business which comes to their firm because of their public life. The lawyer is well trained to serve as a legislator, not only because he is familiar with statutes and court decisions, but also because his training prepares him for becoming an advocate for persons in all walks of life. Yet it would appear that Congress, as well as other legislative bodies, would benefit by having a more widely diversified representation of persons from other professions and occupational groups.

The Constitution requires that a member of the House must be at least twenty-five years of age, reside in the state from which he is elected, and have been a citizen for seven years. Public opinion and tradition ordinarily require also that he be a resident of the district from which he is elected, but there is no legal requirement to this effect. The average age of members of the House of Representatives according to a recent study was 52 years.[3] The age of members has tended to increase since the Civil War, and the average length of

[3] George B. Galloway, *The Legislative Process in Congress,* Thomas Y. Crowell Company, New York, 1953, p. 371.

service has increased very greatly. In 1870 the average member had served 1.04 prior terms of office, while in 1947 he had served, on the average, 4.5 terms. This trend has doubtless been due to the increased compensation, prestige, and power of the office, and also to the tendency for more and more members to make service in Congress a full-time occupation.

Does the House of Representatives attract well-qualified persons? Do its members stand high in their own businesses or professions, and were they community leaders before being elected to Congress? Opinions about the caliber of members of Congress are necessarily subjective. There is some evidence to indicate that the public does not, as a rule, hold members of Congress in high esteem, but persons who express a low opinion of congressmen in general often express a high opinion of their own congressman. Probably it is safe to say that the average qualifications of members of Congress are higher than the public believes, but are not as high as is desirable in view of the great issues which Congress must decide. Higher salaries have doubtless made service in Congress more attractive to persons of ability, but have also made the position attractive to persons who desire the salary.

THE SPEAKER Formerly the Speaker of the House of Representatives was the single most powerful member of either house of Congress, second only in prestige and power to the President. His powers had grown because of the inability of the House to conduct its work without strong leadership. Until 1912 the Speaker enjoyed three great powers which made him master of the House: (1) he appointed the standing committees and named their chairmen; (2) he appointed the Rules Committee, which ran the House, and served as its chairman; and (3) he could recognize or decline to recognize members who desired the floor. With these powers the Speaker was often referred to as a "czar." As long as the Speaker could name the members of the standing committees he could dictate the course of legislation. Several times he delayed appointing the committees (once for 245 days) until his legislative program had been passed. The last of the Speakers under the old order, "Uncle Joe" Cannon of Illinois, dominated the House for years and dictated what bills it would pass. In 1910 a group of "insurgents" led by George Norris of Nebraska succeeded in having the Speaker stripped of the first two powers. No longer was he permitted to name the members of the standing committees—the selection of which is of such great importance to individual members—or to serve as the chairman of the Rules Committee.

The revolt of 1910 curbed the powers of the Speaker and at the same time strengthened those of the committee chairmen and the Rules Committee. Despite these changes, the Speaker is the recognized leader of his party in the House, and a highly respected and able Speaker, like the late Sam Rayburn of Texas, is able to exert a great deal of influence on the actions of the House, but it is influence rather than power. His only powers today are to assign bills to committees, rule on parliamentary questions, recognize members desiring the floor, and appoint select and conference committees.

THE RULES COMMITTEE   It acts as the screening committee of the House of Representatives, selecting the bills which it will consider and pigeon-holing bills that do not meet with the committee's approval. Under the procedure of the House, most public bills require a special rule, which is brought in by the Rules Committee, before they may be taken up for action. A few bills, such as those relating to finance, are specially privileged and may be taken up without a special rule, but others require the approval of the Rules Committee before they may be acted upon by the House. The customary procedure is for the chairman of a standing committee which has reported a bill to the House to apply to the Rules Committee for a special rule that will bring it up for consideration. If the Rules Committee refuses to report a special rule, the effect ordinarily is to kill the bill. In some instances it conducts hearings on the merits of a pending bill, though the standing committee has already conducted extended hearings, and it is not uncommon for the Rules Committee to require the bill to be revised before permitting it to be considered by the House.

The special rule reported by the Rules Committee greatly affects a bill's chances of passage. Favored bills are reported with a rule that limits the time for debate and imposes strict limitations on amendments that may be offered from the floor; on the other hand, bills that are not favored by the Rules Committee are given a "wide-open" rule that permits lengthy debate and unlimited amendments, thus allowing opponents to talk the bill to death or to defeat it by crippling amendments.

It is apparent that the Rules Committee has vast power over the action of the House. It can prevent a bill from being taken up by the House, even when a majority of its members favor the bill and are ready to vote upon it. The Rules Committee in recent years has blocked action on many important bills, including those on Federal aid to education, minimum wages, public housing, civil rights, the creation

"I said, 'Chin up, there's still hope!'" (Haynie in The Louisville Courier-Journal.*)*

The power of the House Rules Committee was illustrated in 1961, when it blocked consideration in the House of President Kennedy's public school aid bill.

of a Department of Urban Affairs, and others. The committee was dominated for years by a combination of conservative Democrats from the South and conservative Republicans from the North. In 1961, after a bitter struggle between Speaker Rayburn and Rep. Howard Smith of Virginia, chairman of the Rules Committee, the committee was enlarged by three members, thus giving the liberals a majority of one. Until this was done, it seemed unlikely that President Kennedy would be able to have some of the bills in his legislative program brought up for action by the House.

PARTY MACHINERY Each political party holds a party caucus (the Republicans call it a conference) at the opening of each session to elect party officers and to select the party candidate for Speaker. Thereafter the party caucus is called occasionally to discuss legislative measures, but relatively little use is made of it. The majority party caucus elects the majority floor leader, who appoints a number of *whips* to assist him in rounding up party members on important votes, and, in general, to serve as a liaison between the party leadership and the rank and file of members. The majority floor leader and the whips attempt by persuasion and cajolery to secure the adoption of the program approved by the party leaders, or the President's program, if the same party controls the House and the Presidency. The minority party elects a minority floor leader, who also appoints party whips, and directs the opposition. Both parties also use a policy or steering committee, but its influence is slight.

In addition to the party organizations, various informal groups or blocs of like-minded members work together on legislation of mutual interest. Thus, the delegation from each state, irrespective of party ties, combines to work for appropriations and public works of special benefit to the state. Members from the cotton-producing states, the corn belt, the dairy states, and other agricultural areas frequently get together in an attempt to agree upon a concerted program. The liberal Democrats have a special study group that meets regularly, and various other loosely formed informal groups combine to advance legislation of interest to them.

THE SENATE

The United States Senate is by all odds the most powerful upper chamber of any legislature in the world. Its legislative power equals that of the House of Representatives, which is generally not true of other upper chambers, and in addition it enjoys two great powers which it does not share with the House. Its power to approve or disapprove treaties with foreign countries and to confirm or to reject nominations of ambassadors and the principal officers of the State Department gives it a preeminent place in foreign affairs. The President and the State Department maintain close contacts with the powerful Senate Committee on Foreign Relations, consulting its members about important policies and relations with other countries before they are put into effect. In choosing a Secretary of State the first consideration of the President is whether the person of his choice can get along with the leaders of the Senate. It is for this reason that senators are often offered this post.

The power of the Senate to pass upon the President's nominations adds greatly to its authority, as well as to the political patronage wielded by individual senators of the President's party. Under the unwritten rule of "senatorial courtesy," the Senate will reject a nominee who is objected to by a senator from the state where he is to serve. The effect of the rule is to transfer the power of nomination of Federal field officers from the President to the senators of each state, provided they are members of the President's party. This gives the senators important patronage and is a symbol of power in their states. The requirement of confirmation gives the Senate a powerful sanction over the appointments of the President and a control over executive officers which is not enjoyed by the House of Representatives.[4]

FOLKWAYS OF THE SENATE   One perceptive student[5] describes the institutional patriotism expected of members of the Senate thus:

> Senators are expected to believe that they belong to the greatest legislative and deliberative body in the world. They are expected to be a bit suspicious of the President and the bureaucrats and just a little disdainful of the House. They are expected to revere the Senate's personnel, organization, and folkways and to champion them to the outside world.

It has been said, not without exaggeration, that the Senate is the most exclusive club in the world. According to William S. White,[6] there is an "Inner Club" and an "Outer Club" within the Senate. Only senators who abide by the customs of the Senate and are highly respected by their colleagues are accepted into the inner club, usually after a number of years of service. These are the senators of both political parties who virtually run the Senate.

The new member serves an apprenticeship when he enters the Senate. He receives committee assignments to the least important committees, and in the committee room sits at the end of the table. During his first year he is expected to be seen but not heard. Senators who violate this rule incur the displeasure of their colleagues and may never be

---

[4] See Joseph P. Harris, *The Advice and Consent of the Senate*, University of California Press, Berkeley, Calif., 1953.
[5] Donald R. Matthews, *U.S. Senators and Their World*, The University of North Carolina Press, Chapel Hill, N.C., 1960, p. 101.
[6] William S. White, *Citadel: The Story of the U.S. Senate*, Harper & Row, Publishers, Incorporated, New York, 1956, chap. 7.

accepted into the inner circle. They are expected to show respect to their elders and to perform the boring tasks that other senators want to avoid. If they would gain the respect of their colleagues, they need to specialize in certain areas of legislation, to acquire the reputation of being a work horse—not a show horse—and to conform to the customs and traditions of the Senate.

A cardinal rule of the Senate is that members shall always show proper courtesy to other senators. If a senator is called away from Washington at the time an important bill on which he wishes to speak is to be taken up, it will be put over at his request. Senators customarily refer to each other as "the distinguished Senator from _____," or "the able and learned Senator from _____." Senators seldom pass up an opportunity to speak in the highest terms of their colleagues, even those for whom they hold no high regard. Another custom is to follow the rule of reciprocity and help out colleagues who are seeking legislation of benefit to their own states.

OFFICERS   The Vice President does not occupy the same position of power and influence as that of the Speaker of the House. He presides over the session when he is present, but is absent much of the time and votes only if there is a tie. His parliamentary rulings may be overridden by a majority vote. The Senate elects a President pro tempore, who presides in the absence of the Vice President but has little other power. When the Vice President and the President pro tempore are both absent, another member presides.

PARTY OFFICERS   Both political parties hold conferences of all of their members at the beginning of the session to elect party officers and to approve the committee assignments which have been made by the party committee on committees. Party conferences may be called at other times to discuss pending legislation and party policy, but relatively little use is made of them. The most important party officers are the majority floor leader and the corresponding floor leader of the minority party. Each party also has a *whip* who is the assistant to the floor leader. After consulting with the members of the majority party policy committee, the majority floor leader customarily makes the motions concerning when and how long the Senate will be in session and the business to be taken up. His role is thus similar to that of the Rules Committee of the House, but he enjoys far less power. He, or a senator designated to act in his stead, is always present when the Senate is in session and participates freely in debate, often closing the argument for the majority. If the majority leader is adept in negotiation and compromise, a good judge of what is possible, and holds the respect of his colleagues, he may exercise great influence on the course of legislation. To succeed, he must discover and espouse legislation which will hold his party together and at times win votes from the opposition. Among the most able recent majority leaders were Alben Barkley, Robert A. Taft, and Lyndon B. Johnson.

THE COMMITTEE SYSTEM

The real work of Congress is transacted not on the floor of the two chambers but in the committees, which have been called "little legislatures." Because of the increase in the number and importance of the standing subcommittees since 1946, it would be more accurate today to say that the real work of Congress is transacted by the subcommittees. Congress makes greater use of committees and subcommittees than any other legislative body in the world; it grants them greater powers and exercises less control over them than do other legislative bodies.

Congress uses several types of committees. The Senate has 16 *standing* committees and the House has 20. With one or two exceptions, these standing committees are assigned specified areas of legislation for consideration. Thus, each house has committees on foreign relations, appropriations, revenues, armed services, agriculture, judiciary, commerce, labor, and others.

In addition to standing committees, each house uses *special* or *select* committees from time to time, usually to conduct investigations. The use of special committees to conduct investigations has declined since the passage of the Legislative Reorganization Act of 1946, which authorized standing committees to conduct investigations within their jurisdictional areas. Special committees are not usually authorized to recommend legislation, and hence their recommendations are subject to review by standing committees before being brought before the houses of Congress for action. They are terminated when they have completed their assignments.

Joint committees are occasionally used for investigations and other purposes. The leading example is the Joint Committee on Atomic Energy, which is a standing committee of Congress. The intense jealousy of its prerogatives evidenced by each house prevents wider use of joint standing committees.

Conference committees are established when the House and Senate fail to agree on the provisions of a bill. Most important bills are sent to conference committees, which consist of the highest-ranking members in both parties of the standing committees which reported the bill. The conference committees, which meet in closed sessions, wield a great deal of power. They often make substantial changes in bills, although under the rules they are not permitted to introduce new provisions except to compromise the differences in the bill as it passed the two houses.

Most standing committees utilize *subcommittees*, in some instances as many as 10 or more. The Senate subcommittees are established on a continuing basis and operate from one Congress to another, but those of the House are established at the beginning of each Congress. Some subcommittees are granted a large measure of autonomy and operate very much like independent committees, with their own staffs and committee rooms. This is especially true of the appropriations subcommittees, whose recommendations are rarely changed by the parent committee. The centers of power in each house have partially shifted from the committee chairmen to the chairmen of subcommittees.

Every member of Congress seeks assignment to one of the major committees, especially the "bread-and-butter" committees whose activities relate to his own district or state. Western congressmen often seek assignment to the Interior or Public Works Committees, which pass upon public works projects and programs of interest to the West; those from agricultural areas want to be assigned to the Agriculture Committee; others seek an assignment to the Appropriations Committee, because of the great power that it wields, or to the Rules Committee of the House. The Foreign Relations Committee of the Senate ranks first in the order of member preference in the Senate, followed in order by the Appropriations, Finance, Armed Services, and Agriculture Committees.[7] In the House, the ranking of committees in order of preference is similar to that in the Senate. The two committees which rank lowest in membership preference in each house are those on the District of Columbia, and the Post Office and Civil Service.

Committee assignments in each house are made by a committee on committees of each party. In the House the Democratic members of the Ways and Means Committee act as a party committee on committees, while the Republicans utilize a special committee on committees consisting of one member from each state that has a Republican repre-

[7] See Donald R. Matthews, *op. cit.*, p. 148.

sentative. Freshmen members of both houses are usually assigned to the least desirable committees, but there are some exceptions. As Democratic majority leader of the Senate, Lyndon Johnson insisted that each freshman Democratic senator should receive one "good" committee assignment, a practice that has continued. Members of the Senate serve on two or three standing committees, while members of the House serve on one or two. Both senators and representatives, however, serve on a much larger number of subcommittees.

COMMITTEE CHAIRMEN The chairmen of standing committees are the real leaders of Congress, though their powers have declined with the increasing use of subcommittees. The chairman is invariably the senior ranking member of the majority party in length of service on the committee, and is usually highly respected by his colleagues. Because of his prestige and the great power that he wields, he is usually able to control the actions of the committee. Some chairmen rule with an iron hand, even refusing to permit consideration of bills to which they are opposed, but most chairmen act in a more democratic and responsible manner.

The chairman selects the members of the committee staff (except for those assigned to serve the minority members) and directs their work. He also, after consulting with other members of the committee, determines which bills the committee will consider. He appoints the subcommittees and assigns bills to them for consideration. Although seniority is a prime consideration in the selection of the subcommittee chairmen, the chairman of the committee has some discretion and can usually pick members who will follow his lead. Often he appoints himself to the most important subcommittee chairmanships. He manages the debate on bills reported by the committee, or names another member to be floor manager. He heads the conference committees for such bills and selects the other members who serve with him.

Most committee chairmen have served 10 or more years on the committee and through long and continuous service have acquired a great deal of knowledge about the legislation within its jurisdiction. In addition, they make it their business to become informed about major bills before the committee, and can turn to the committee staff for research or assistance. Although at times the chairman is overruled by the committee, such cases are rare. Members of the committee, who may later seek favors that only the chairman can grant, are reluctant to oppose his wishes.

The rule of seniority in selecting committee chairmen often elevates to these important posts of leadership persons of advanced age, sometimes persons of limited ability, and not infrequently those who are not in sympathy with the policies of their own party. The chairmen of major committees usually come from safe constituencies in one-party sections of the country. When the Democrats are in power, the large majority of committee chairmen come from the South and the Southwest, and when the Republicans control Congress, they come from the solidly Republican states in the farm belt of the Midwest and New England. Regardless of which party is in power, the large urban centers command few of the major chairmanships. Thus, the positions of greatest power usually go to members from rural, one-party areas that are relatively unaffected by the movements and issues that agitate the large cities. This accounts for the essential conservatism of Congress, regardless of which party is in power.

Review Questions

1. Discuss the various functions of Congress and comment on their importance.

2. What is the gerrymander? Explain the overrepresentation of rural population in the House of Representatives. What will be the effect of the Supreme Court decision in *Baker v. Carr?*

3. Why is the high cost of election campaigns a serious problem in American public life?

4. What services do members of Congress render to their constituents? Discuss the effects of this practice.

5. What powers did the Speaker have before 1910 that enabled him to be the "czar" of the House? What powers and influence does he have today?

6. What are the powers of the House Rules Committee and what effect does it have on legislative policies?

7. Describe the party organization of the House and the Senate. How is party discipline maintained?

8. Describe the committee system in Congress and discuss the principal criticisms. What are the powers of committee chairmen?

THE LEGISLATIVE PROCESS

Chapter 5

THE ORIGIN OF BILLS

Few of the fifteen thousand bills introduced in each Congress are the brain-children of its members. The majority are initiated by the executive departments, private organizations, or individual citizens. A few are proposed by the President as a part of his legislative program. It is easy to have a bill introduced, but very difficult to secure its enactment. There is no limit on the number of bills which members of Congress may introduce. Members often introduce bills at the request of constituents or others without any intention of pressing for enactment, at times marking such bills to indicate that they were introduced "by request." Thereafter it is up to the initiating group to drum up support and seek a committee hearing on their bill. Only about a thousand bills are passed by each Congress; the vast majority never emerge from the "dim dungeons of silence" of the committee to which they are assigned.

Public bills relate to public affairs, while *private bills* affect only named persons. The latter are used mostly to pay claims of citizens against the government that are not legally allowable in the court of claims. *Joint resolutions*, which have the same effect as statutes, are used for actions of a nonpermanent character. Public bills, which are by far the most important, vary greatly in scope and importance. Most bills amend existing statutes, but others propose new legislation. The large majority are noncontroversial and those that reach the floor are passed without opposition. Usually less than two dozen bills of major importance are taken up in each session of Congress.

Congress increasingly looks to the President to submit a legislative program and devotes most of its attention to his proposals. Formerly protocol limited the President to general recommendations of policy, leaving the drafting of bills to members of Congress. Jealous of its prerogatives, Congress once returned a petty bill submitted by President Lincoln with a request that it be passed, declining even to consider it. Formerly bills to carry out the President's recommendations were bootlegged to friendly members of Congress to be introduced as their own, without indicating the source, but today Congress expects the President or the department primarily concerned to submit draft bills to carry out his recommendations. The administration bills are freely revised by Congress and often the final acts bear little resemblance to the original drafts.

Each executive department normally submits to Congress at each session a number of legislative requests, the most important of which may be included in the President's legislative program. The President must be careful, however, not to support too many measures, which would lessen the effect of his endorsements and weaken his role as legislative leader.

One of the most important responsibilities of executive departments is to recommend needed legislation relating to the functions assigned to them. Most of their legislative requests are designed to improve administrative operations, but they also recommend legislation authorizing new policies and programs. The departments are usually well-equipped to make recommendations on needed legislation relating to their assigned functions, for their officers are well-informed about problems, operations, and public needs, and are able to draw upon the technical and legal staff. Department officials, however, must guard against becoming too zealous in advocating their proposed legislation, or they will be criticized for lobbying. A 1919 statute prohibits departments from attempting to influence legislation, and although the statute is not enforced, it acts as a restraint on their legislative activities.

During the preparation of bills departmental officials usually consult with various interested organizations and congressional leaders, as well as with other executive departments that may be concerned. At this stage compromises and revisions are often made that will greatly facilitate the passage of the bill. If an agreement is not reached, proposed legislation is almost certain to be opposed and will likely be defeated or greatly revised by Congress.

Departmental bills must be "cleared" by the Legislative Reference Division of the Bureau of the Budget to make sure that they are in conformity with the President's program and policies, and to assure that other interested departments have been consulted. Many department bills affect other departments in one way or another. Advance consultation permits any differences of opinion to be reconciled prior to submission of a bill and thus avoids interdepartmental fights before congressional committees. Legislation of major interest to several departments is often prepared under the direction of an interdepartmental committee.[1]

Although in other countries it is the practice for all important legislation to be proposed by the executive departments, individual members of Congress play an important though a declining role in the initiation of legislation. Many major laws are first proposed by members of Congress, and, after they acquire widespread support, are included in the President's legislative program. Thus, Sen. George Norris advocated a public power program in the Tennessee Valley for years before President Roosevelt came to office and made it a part of his New Deal program. Other New Deal measures were also pushed in Congress by groups of members for several years before President Roosevelt put them on his "must" list. It should be noted that many important bills are enacted without the President's support, and, at times, despite his opposition.

[1] Richard E. Neustadt, "The Presidency and Legislation: The Growth of Central Clearance," *American Political Science Review*, 1954, vol. 47, pp. 641–71.

TO HAVE OR NOT TO HAVE A BILL? "The legislative process is only one of the methods through which the contestants in the social struggle pursue their objectives," writes a perceptive student of the legislative process.[2] The same objective may often be achieved either through administrative action or legislation, or possibly through judicial action, though usually with somewhat different results. The organization or group desiring a course of action must weigh the cost, time required, likelihood of success, and probable effects of each method. Some results can be achieved only by legislation. All department programs and activities must be authorized by law; no appropriation can be made until an activity is authorized. Before a new program may be instituted, an act must be passed authorizing the activity, usually specifying the objectives and defining the operations to be carried on, and perhaps limiting the amount of funds that may be expended.

Departments sometimes seek new authorizing legislation although they could initiate action under the authority of existing laws. Specific authorization of a new program arms the administrator with a congressional mandate which helps him to secure funds. President Eisenhower had ample constitutional authority to send armed forces to the Middle East and to the waters around Formosa, but he sought and secured advance congressional approval to strengthen his hand. Bills not requested by departments are sometimes introduced to spur executive officers to exercise authority that they already have, or to exercise it more vigorously. The threat of such a law may produce the desired results without its passage.

Government departments hesitate to seek legislation unless there is an imperative need, and often get along with statutory provisions and restrictions that seriously hamper their work, fearing that Congress may write in provisions that they do not want. The difficulties of securing the passage of a bill are so great that standing committees are usually unwilling to bother with corrective legislation unless the need is urgent.

Bills are often introduced as a publicity device, as a rallying point for advocates of a government policy. Congress considers only specific legislative proposals; in order to secure consideration of a new policy or program, it must be put in the form of a bill. If proponents can persuade a committee to hold public hearings, they may secure nationwide publicity that would not be available in any other way. Bills are

[2] Bertram Gross, *The Legislative Struggle,* McGraw-Hill Book Company, Inc., New York, 1953, p. 153.

often introduced without any expectation that they will be passed, but to gain public support for a policy or program that may eventually lead to legislation.

THE LEGISLATIVE STRUGGLE

The administration bills proposed by the President and those requested by the executive departments have a much better chance of passage than bills without such support. They are virtually assured of being considered, while bills that are sponsored by private organizations and introduced by individual members, unless they have strong backing, are likely never to be considered. The President's bills are submitted to Congress with a special message which explains and defends his policy recommendations and states forcefully the need for the legislation. His message is reported in the daily press throughout the country, and is reproduced in full in *The New York Times* and in some other leading dailies. It is followed by editorial comments, usually favorable at this stage, and enterprising reporters interview leading members of both houses to publicize their views on the President's proposals.

To secure the adoption of his legislative program the President personally confers with the leaders of his party in both houses, the chairmen and ranking members of the committees, and other members of Congress whose support is needed. He is aided by a small liaison staff of persons who are widely and favorably known "on the Hill," whose function is to keep the President informed about congressional opinion and to aid congressional leaders in lining up the necessary support. The President, however, looks to the department primarily concerned with each bill to explain and defend it before Congress.[3]

Department bills that are not included in the President's legislative program have many of the same advantages as administration bills. Every department has many strong supporters and friends among members of Congress, who usually support its legislative requests. In addition, departments are often able to enlist the active support of powerful interest groups, which are usually consulted in the preparation of bills. Department bills, however, must run the legislative gantlet and if they are controversial, will face strong opposition within Congress and by outside interest groups.

Bills sponsored by individual members, usually at the behest of outside groups and organizations, commonly face a much more difficult

[3] The President's role as legislative leader is discussed in greater detail in chap. 3.

course. Without the publicity available to the President and to the executive departments, such bills have great difficulty in attracting national attention. Members pushing such legislation often try to secure the support, or at least acquiescence, of the administration. Bills that have the active support of leading members of Congress and powerful private organizations, however, are as likely to be passed as administration bills, especially if they have no strong opposition.

COMMITTEE HEARINGS   The first public test of a bill comes when hearings are conducted by the standing committee to which it is referred. If it is an important administration bill, the secretary of the department concerned will usually appear as the first witness. After his opening statement concerning the broad objectives of the bill, he is questioned by committee members, probably about the parts of the bill that are more likely to be opposed. He is followed by other department witnesses who are more familiar with the details of the bill. After the department witnesses have finished, representatives of private organizations, both pro and con, are called to testify, usually at their request. The testimony is taken down in shorthand and subsequently a verbatim transcript is published. Both proponents and opponents attempt during

The steps by which a bill becomes a law. Bills may be introduced in either house.

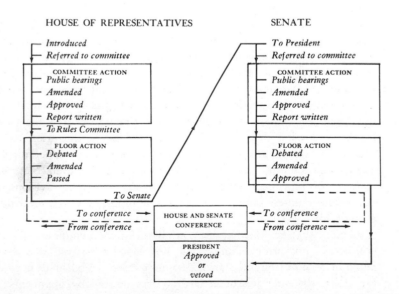

the hearings to build a record that can be used in later debates. If the bill is important, the hearings may extend over days or even weeks.

The members of the committee customarily take a leading part in the hearings and their questions and comments indicate their own positions. If a member agrees with a witness, he often asks him leading questions and adds comments of his own. On the other hand, committee members who disagree with a witness may attempt to discredit his testimony. Most committee members have already made up their minds about the proposed legislation and use the hearings not to gain further information, but rather to build up a record favorable to their point of view. The statements of the leading witnesses on both sides are usually highly informing, but the value of the hearings is often lessened by repetitious and sometimes irrelevant questions.

Because of the obvious shortcomings of public hearings as a means of exploring the policy issues involved in proposed legislation, departments and outside organizations commonly submit written and often lengthy statements of their views, and the hearings are also supplemented by special studies conducted by the committee staff or outside consultants. Congressional committees do not suffer from any lack of data and opinions on pending legislation, most of it one-sided. Their task is that of sifting the evidence, weighing the issues, and assessing the strengths of the competing forces. This is preeminently the task of the politician—the representative elected by the people to decide upon public policies.

After the public hearings are concluded, the committee goes into *executive*, that is, closed sessions to deliberate on the bill and to revise it section by section before it is reported. Executive sessions are attended only by members of the committee and its staff, and others on invitation. It is not uncommon for department experts to be asked to attend some of the executive sessions in order to be available for further questioning. Members of the committee are able to express their views frankly, knowing that they will not be quoted in the press. At this stage compromises are worked out and decisions made concerning the provisions of the bill; often an entirely new bill is drafted. No record is made of how each member votes on the various provisions, but committee deliberations are often leaked to the press, frequently in garbled form.

The bill that emerges represents the will of the committee, the give and take of compromise, and, if it is not always improved, it is at least made more politically acceptable. In most cases the bill does not go as far as its advocates wish, but farther than desired by opponents. Although administration bills are thus often "watered down" by the committee, they are usually accepted by the department in the hope that the second house can be persuaded to restore important provisions that have been omitted or trimmed.

THE ROLE OF PRESSURE GROUPS   A leading part in the legislative struggle is played by private organizations of all kinds, which are usually called "pressure groups" or "interest groups."[4] Because of the ability of such organizations to influence the course of legislation, especially to block legislation to which they are opposed, the terms "pressure groups" and "interest groups" are often used in a derogatory sense. The power which they wield, especially when several pressure groups work together, constitutes one of the major problems of democratic government. As a rule, they represent producers, while the great body of consumers is unorganized. A small body of men who have definite and specific interests of great concern to them, and who know exactly what they want and how to go about getting it, is more powerful than a large body of unorganized persons with less direct interest.

Yet the existence of private associations is inevitable in modern society. They are one of the principal means by which legislative bodies are informed of the wishes and desires of the great mass of citizens. They perform a useful, even indispensable, function of supplying legislators with information about policies and legislation under consideration. Their representatives, who like to be called "legislative counsel" or "legislative advocates" instead of lobbyists, are usually persons of ability and integrity. Legislators soon learn that they can rely upon the information supplied to them by the representatives of the leading interest groups.

Members of the "third house," as they are often called, are better paid, as a rule, than legislators. Many of them are former members of the legislative body. They have expert staffs which are usually better-informed than congressional staffs. Pressure groups follow all legislation affecting their members, and occasionally sponsor bills, though their role is primarily defensive. They keep their members informed about all relevant legislation so that organized opposition or support may be delivered when needed. The more influential pressure groups have highly effective intelligence systems, and have detailed information

[4] See David Truman, *The Governmental Process*, Alfred A. Knopf, Inc., New York, 1953; Donald Blaisdell, *American Democracy Under Pressure*, The Ronald Press Company, New York, 1957; Bertram Gross, *op. cit.*, especially chaps. 2 and 3.

concerning the provisions and probable effects of bills that are of concern to their members, but also how much support each bill has, whether it is likely to pass, how it may best be defeated or amended, which members favor it, which are opposed, and which are undecided. Consequently, their campaigns are skillfully directed to gain the votes of particular members who can be influenced.

The legislative representatives of pressure groups appear before committees and present well-organized and informed arguments for or against pending bills, usually couched in terms of the national interest rather than their special interests. Their most effective work, however, is behind the scenes in private conversations with individual legislators. In important legislative struggles, the heat is also turned on key members of Congress by local organizations and prominent citizens back home. A telephone call from a leading banker in the congressman's own district or from a prominent local industrialist or labor leader carries great weight, especially from persons who have made substantial contributions to the campaign fund of the congressman.

Private organizations also use other devices to influence legislative action. Large-scale publicity campaigns may be conducted to influence public opinion, as, for example, the campaigns conducted by the American Medical Association against health insurance and the proposed medical care program for the aged, or that of organized labor against the Taft-Hartley Act. Catchy slogans and epithets are often used in these campaigns. Thus, a bill to outlaw labor-management agreements for the closed shop is called "the right to work" bill; health insurance is denounced as "socialized medicine," and the Taft-Hartley Act is referred to as the "Slave-labor Act."

Pressure organizations are most effective in propagandizing among their own members, and their lobbying activities are most effective with their own friends in Congress. Members of Congress are not neutral judges who weigh the evidence and pass upon legislative contests in a judicial manner. "What are the different classes of legislators," asked James Madison in *The Federalist* (No. 10), "but advocates and parties to the causes which they determine?" A leading authority on Congress[5] has written recently:

> Today many of our legislators are little more than lobbyists in disguise for organized interests back home: cotton, tobacco, steel and textiles, cattle and

[5] George B. Galloway, *The Legislative Process in Congress*, Thomas Y. Crowell Company, New York, 1953, p. 514.

wool, and the like. They do not wait for pressure from their districts, but are prepared with speeches and briefs, amendments and arguments, to protect local and sectional interests.

CONTROL OF LOBBYING   Title III of the Legislative Reorganization Act of 1946 requires organizations and individuals whose *principal* activity is to influence legislation to register with the Clerk of the House of Representatives and the Clerk of the Senate, and to file financial statements of receipts and expenditures, including the purposes for which money was expended and the legislation they are paid to support or oppose. The limitation that only persons whose *principal* activity is lobbying are required to register provides a large loophole, permitting many to escape complying with the law. The act does not regulate lobbying as such, but merely seeks to require public disclosure of lobbying activities. It has been subject to much litigation.

In 1953 the Supreme Court held that the term "lobbying activities" meant direct representation before Congress, and not indirect attempts to exert influence on legislation through a publicity campaign (*United States v. Rumeley*, 345 U.S. 41). This decision provides a second large loophole, for much lobbying activity is carried on through publicity campaigns. Congress has the power to regulate lobbying in any form and to require financial reports on lobbying activities, but it has not revised the law to require public disclosure of lobbying expenditures. A select committee of the House of Representatives which conducted an investigation of lobbying in 1950 recommended numerous changes in the law to make it more effective,[6] and a special committee of the Senate made similar recommendations.[7] However, no action has been taken.

PROCEDURE IN THE HOUSE

The rules of procedure of the House, which have developed over the years, are extremely elaborate. Not only has the House adopted and revised from time to time its rules, which are set forth in the House Manual, but the rulings of the Speaker and the chairmen of the Committee of the Whole constitute precedents which govern its deliberations. These rulings have been published in an 11-volume work, *Hind's*

[6] *General Interim Report*, H.R. 1085, 1950, and *Report and Recommendations on Federal Lobbying Act*, H.R. 3239, 1951.
[7] *Final Report*, 85th Cong., 1st Sess., S. Report 395, 1957.

and Cannon's Precedents of the House of Representatives. Only a few of the more important procedures will be discussed here.

Bills are introduced merely by sending them to the clerk's desk. The House does not permit joint sponsorship of bills, as is the practice in the Senate, and hence identical bills may be introduced by two or more members. House bills bear the letters "H.R." and the number of the bill, while Senate bills are designated by the letter "S." and the number. After introduction, bills are referred by the Speaker to the proper committee, usually on advice of the Parliamentarian. If a bill is approved by the standing committee to which it is referred, usually after numerous revisions, it is reported back to the House and is placed on one of the several calendars of bills. Finance bills are placed on the *Union Calendar*, and, being privileged, may be called up for consideration by the chairman of the committee when he is recognized (by prearrangement) by the Speaker. Other public bills are placed on the *House Calendar;* private bills are placed on the *Private Calendar;* and noncontroversial bills may be transferred to the *Consent Calendar.* Certain days are set aside for the consideration of the latter two calendars. A bill is normally taken from the Union Calendar or the House Calendar, not when it is reached in order, but when a special rule is brought in by the Rules Committee making it the order of the day. Such a rule calls for immediate consideration of the bill, and usually establishes special rules governing its consideration, including the amount of time that will be allotted for debate and limitations on the amendments that may be offered.

Standing committees often kill bills by refusing to report them to the House for its consideration. If a majority of the members of the House favor a bill that is being held by a standing committee, they can force it out of committee and bring it before the House for its consideration by submitting a petition to discharge the committee from further consideration of the bill, but the rules and the traditions of the House make this procedure very difficult. An *absolute* majority of all members (218) must sign such a petition, and a majority of those present must vote to take up the bill when it is brought before the House seven days later. Members of the House are reluctant to act on a bill until after it has been considered by the standing committee to which it is referred, and hence it is rarely possible to secure 218 signers to a discharge petition. The threat of a discharge petition, however, is often sufficient to force a committee to report on a bill that it is holding. If the rules were amended to make it easier to discharge standing committees from further consideration of bills referred to them, the effect would be to make them more responsive to the wishes of a majority of members of the House.

In considering most bills the House resolves itself into the *Committee of the Whole*. When the House is in regular session, the Speaker presides and a majority of all members (218) must be present to constitute a quorum for the transaction of business. When the House resolves itself into the Committee of the Whole the Speaker withdraws and another member he has designated presides. Only 100 members are required to constitute a quorum in the Committee of the Whole, and the procedure is more informal than when the House is in regular session. When the Committee of the Whole has completed its work for the day, it resolves itself into formal session, and the Speaker returns to the chair.

Votes in the House are taken in four ways: by a voice vote; by division, in which members stand and are counted by the presiding officer; by teller count, in which members file through the aisle and are counted by tellers; and by a roll call. Roll call votes are not used in the Committee of the Whole, but may be required by one-fifth of those present when the House is in regular session. This is one of the reasons for extensive use of the Committee of the Whole, which avoids a record vote on controversial amendments. When the roll is called, electric bells ring in the House office buildings to enable members who are in their offices to come to the chamber in time to be recorded. Roll call votes, each of which requires about three-quarters of an hour, take up a vast amount of time of the House during each session. Many state legislatures have installed electric voting which permits a roll call vote to be taken and recorded in less than a minute, but the House has been unwilling to do likewise, for this would make it necessary for members to be in constant attendance when the House is in session lest they miss roll call votes.

The time allotted for debate in the House is strictly controlled. For more than a hundred years the House has limited the time during which any member may speak to one hour, but speeches of this length are practically unknown because of the limited time allowed for debate of even the most important measures. The rule under which a bill is brought up limits the time allowed for debate, one-half being allotted to members favoring the bill and one-half to opponents. Customarily the chairman of the committee reporting the bill, or another member designated by him, has charge of the time allocated for proponents, and the time of opponents is controlled by the ranking minority member of the committee. The largest amount of time is taken by members of the committee reporting the bill, and the remaining time is divided among others who wish to speak. Often members who are granted limited time ask permission to extend their remarks in the record.

The quality of the debate in the House leaves much to be desired. Visitors to the galleries are often shocked at the small attendance when routine business is being conducted, but many members of Congress find it necessary to be absent at such times in order to take care of more important work on committees and to handle the requests of constituents. At times the debate is lively, pertinent, and well-attended, especially when the debate on important bills nears a close and the party leaders on each side make the closing statements. The debate on amendments in the Committee of the Whole, during which speakers are limited to five minutes, moves at a rapid pace and those who speak are usually well-informed, but at other times the debate is not impressive. Many speeches on the floor are designed for home consumption. Few votes are changed by the debates; when in doubt most members rely largely upon the judgment of the committee members of their party rather than upon speeches on the floor.

Debate is virtually a lost art in the House, due in large part to the severe time limitations placed on it. When only a few hours are allowed to debate an important and complex measure, and the allotted time is divided among many members who want to express their views, no member has sufficient time to discuss the various provisions of the bill with any degree of thoroughness. Aware of these limitations, as well as of the fact that debates seldom influence votes, members are not encouraged to prepare for them, and the debates often degenerate into platitudes and clichés, with frequent pleas for support of the President, the party, or the leadership.

PROCEDURE IN THE SENATE

The Senate, a much smaller body than the House of Representatives, is able to transact its business more informally and without strict rules of procedure. Much of its business is transacted under suspension of the rules by unanimous consent. The Senate does not operate under special rules, as the House does. The Senate Committee on Rules does not act as a screening body to select the bills that will be brought before the Senate for its consideration. The Senate itself decides which bills it will take up. By custom, motions to take up particular bills are made by the majority leader, but may be made by others. The majority leader does not have the power to prevent a bill from being considered, but he has a great deal of influence in determining the order in which bills are considered.

The Senate standing committees do not have the same power as House committees to bottle up bills and prevent them from coming before the chamber for consideration. A Senate committee can be discharged from the consideration of a bill by a motion on the floor, which may be passed by a simple majority vote. Yet there is a strong tradition against recalling a bill from a committee, and discharge motions are seldom passed. The fact that such a motion may be made and passed by a majority of those present and voting, however, prevents Senate committees from arbitrarily pigeonholing bills that a majority of senators favor.

The Senate acts on measures without the use of a committee of the whole. It does not use several calendars as does the House, but all reported bills are placed on the Calendar of the Senate, from which they may be taken up for consideration by a majority vote. Custom and tradition have greater influence than formal rules, though the Senate has a large body of rules which were first compiled by Thomas Jefferson when he was Vice President.

THE FILIBUSTER   One of the most notable features of Senate procedure is that the rules permit unlimited debate. With certain exceptions, a senator on being recognized may hold the floor as long as he desires and is able to remain standing. He does not have to confine his remarks to the subject before the chamber, but may speak on wholly irrelevant matters. The absence of the requirement of relevance often leads to a disconnected debate on important legislation. During the debate on a major bill a member may secure the floor and make a speech on the beauties of his home state or anything else that he wishes to talk about; the Senate quickly empties, except for two or three members who wearily wait until the debate can be resumed. This kind of irrelevant debate is frowned upon by the members of the "Inner Club."

The Senate prides itself on being the only major legislative chamber in the world that has no rules restricting the length of time members may speak. Yet time limits are in fact placed on debate, for only by adopting such restrictions can any legislative body transact its business. After debate on a bill has proceeded for several days and the principal proponents and opponents have made lengthy speeches, the majority leader is usually able to secure a unanimous agreement fixing a time when debate will end and the Senate will proceed to vote on the bill and all amendments. By this time everything that can be said for and against the bill has probably been said, and further continuation of the debate would be tedious.

In the early history of the Senate the rules permitted the previous question to be moved, the usual device for closing debate, but this rule was dropped in 1806 and thereafter until 1917 there was no provision whereby a majority could bring debate to an end and force a vote to be taken. Prior to 1841 little use was made of the filibuster, that is, prolonged debate, to prevent a vote from being taken. After a prolonged filibuster in 1841, however, Henry Clay proposed the adoption of a one-hour rule, saying, "Let our contests be of intellectuality, and not of physical force in seeing who could sit out the other or consume the most time in useless debate."[8]

Prior to 1933, when the second or "short" session of Congress ended on March 4, the filibuster (which prevents other business from being transacted) was highly effective in the closing days of the session. Individual senators often resorted to the filibuster to secure appropriations for their states, holding the floor until the Senate leaders agreed to yield to their demands. Sen. Ben Tillman of South Carolina conducted a filibuster in 1903 to force the Senate to include an item in the appropriation bill to pay a claim of his state. Securing the floor a few hours before the Senate was required to adjourn, he proceeded to read from Byron's *Childe Harold* until his colleagues agreed to the item. Similarly Senator Stone of Missouri once conducted a filibuster to force an appropriation for a new post office building in St. Louis.

In 1908 the elder Sen. Robert M. La Follette of Wisconsin led a filibuster against the Vreeland-Aldrich Currency Bill, which lasted 28 days but finally failed.

In 1917 a filibuster of 11 senators blocked the passage of a bill urged by President Wilson to authorize the arming of merchant vessels. The United States was still neutral and the filibustering senators feared that the passage of the bill would lead the country into World War I. The House had passed the bill with only a few dissenting votes. President Wilson made a historic attack[9] on the 11 filibustering senators and the rules of the Senate which permitted a few members to block action in a crisis:

[8] Quoted by Lindsay Rogers, *The American Senate*, F. S. Crofts & Co., New York, 1926, p. 166.
[9] *The Washington Post*, March 15, 1917.

> The Senate of the United States is the only legislative body in the world which cannot act when a majority is ready for action. A little group of willful men, representing no opinion but their own, have rendered the great government of the United States helpless and contemptible. . . . The only remedy is that the rules of the Senate shall be so altered that it can act.

Four days later the Senate adopted a cloture rule under which 16 senators may petition to limit debate and if a two-thirds majority vote in favor of cloture, members of the Senate are limited thereafter to one hour each. The cloture rule has continued in effect, though subsequently modified, but has been successfully invoked only five times in 45 years. Numerous attempts have been made at other times to invoke cloture, but have failed to secure the required two-thirds majority.

A successful filibuster requires the concerted efforts of a group of senators who are able to prolong debate by lengthy speeches and dilatory tactics until the majority of the Senate agrees to table the measure under consideration, in order that essential legislation may be taken up. Filibustering senators usually make little pretense of speaking on the bill before the Senate; with their desks piled high with books and papers, they talk or read on any subject of their choosing. Fellow senators often help out by asking lengthy questions, which may take a half hour or even longer, thus providing the senator who has the floor with a "breather." Another delaying tactic is for a colleague to observe to the presiding officer that a quorum is not present; this requires a quorum call to bring in a majority of senators before the debate may be resumed. During filibusters the Senate is often held in continuous sessions in an attempt to wear out the filibustering senators and force them to yield the floor. The struggle becomes one of endurance until one side gives way.

In recent years the filibuster has been used principally by Southern senators to block votes on civil rights legislation, including bills relating to the right to vote, segregation, lynching, and fair employment practices. Senators favoring civil rights legislation have tried unsuccessfully to amend the rules to permit a majority of senators present and voting to impose cloture. Regardless of the rules, it is difficult to invoke cloture, as the experience of the last 45 years indicates, for the majority of senators are reluctant to vote any limitation on debate.

"Our position has been misrepresented. We only want to deny the U.S. Senate the right to vote." (Herblock in The Washington Post & Times Herald.)

The right of unlimited debate has on occasion been used by senators to present the issues and extend the debate until the public became informed and until the force of public opinion could be brought to bear on the outcome. Thus, a small group of liberal senators carried on an extended debate in 1962 in opposition to the administration bill to set up a private corporation to develop and operate a space-satellite communication system. For the first time in 35 years the Senate adopted a cloture rule to limit debate. On numerous occasions senators have thus been able to force the adoption of important amendments to pending bills. Senators who have spoken at great length against bills which they regard as contrary to public interest contend that a lengthy speech on the merits of a bill, which is intended to inform the country and to delay but not prevent a vote from being taken, is not a filibuster, for the purpose of a filibuster is to prevent a pending bill or motion from coming to a vote.

The filibuster enables a determined minority of senators to prevent legislation which they regard as obnoxious from coming to a vote. Its effect is to require not merely a majority of the Senate, but a concurrent majority of senators from all major sections of the country to approve proposed legislation. The Constitution protects the rights of minorities as well as of majorities. A group of senators large enough to carry on a successful filibuster and sufficiently determined to withstand the pressure of public opinion can prevent the government from taking an action that their section regards as unacceptable.

The right of members to speak without limit is a highly prized tradition of the Senate and one that it is reluctant to give up. When wisely used by senators who are thoroughly prepared and speak on issues of national importance, their lengthy speeches serve to educate the country and to arouse public opinion; however, such speeches are frequently made by senators whose loquacity exceeds their sagacity. The senators who have the greatest influence on the course of legislation rarely speak at length. It is the function of legislative bodies not only to debate but also to act. Action without debate is unwise and dangerous; debate without action is futile and renders the government impotent in dealing with the pressing problems of society. One of the principal causes of the rise of dictatorships in other countries has been the public distrust and disgust with a legislative body that can only talk but cannot act when events demand action.

Review Questions

1. What are the major sources of bills in Congress? Is the growing trend for the most important bills to be submitted by the President and the executive departments desirable? Why or why not?

2. Why is it required that department bills be cleared by the Legislative Reference Division of the Bureau of the Budget?

3. Why are bills often introduced in Congress without expectation of passage?

4. Describe the procedure followed by standing committees in considering bills.

5. Discuss the role of pressure groups in the legislative process. In what ways are they constructive?

6. What regulations apply to lobbying before Congress? Why are they ineffective?

7. Describe the procedure of the House of Representatives in considering bills. Why is debate a lost art in the House?

8. Discuss the discharge rule in the House and its importance. Has it been an effective remedy?

9. Compare procedure of the Senate with that of the House. How are minorities able to obstruct legislation?

10. Discuss the filibuster in the Senate, its uses, effects, and arguments pro and con. Trace the history and operation of the cloture rule.

CONGRESS: THE GRAND INQUEST OF THE NATION

Chapter 6

"We are called the Grand Inquest of the Nation," said William Pitt in the British House of Commons in 1742, "and as such it is our duty to inquire into every step of publick management, either Abroad or at Home, in order to see that nothing has been done amiss." The title may be applied even more appropriately to Congress today, for it devotes most of its time to conducting investigations and watching over the administration. These two major functions of Congress are considered in this chapter, which also deals with recent movements to reorganize and strengthen the Congress so that it may be better equipped to cope with the heavy responsibilities placed upon it in the second half of the twentieth century.

THE CONDUCT OF INVESTIGATIONS

The conduct of investigations has become one of the major activities of Congress, and the one that often receives greater public attention than all others. It conducts investigations not only to acquire information to serve as the basis for legislation, but also to check on the administration of the laws. The first investigation, which was conducted during Washington's first term of office, was to ascertain the reasons for the disastrous defeat of a military expedition. Since that date in 1792 there have been few if any sessions of Congress that did not witness one or more investigations of the conduct of the executive departments. At present Congress conducts over a hundred separate investigations at each session of Congress.

Prior to 1946 it was necessary in each house to secure a resolution authorizing an investigation before it could be undertaken, but the Legislative Reorganization Act of that year authorized all standing committees to conduct investigations, which have since grown by leaps and bounds. The House, however, has granted permanent authority to subpoena witnesses and to require the production of papers to only four standing committees; the others must secure a resolution authorizing these powers for each investigation. Authorizing resolutions are also required by the House before special funds are voted for the conduct of investigations. Its committees, however, have substantial regular appropriations which may be used for the conduct of investigations.

Congress also conducts investigations to inform the public, even though the facts may be well known to the lawmakers. During the thirties a famous investigation was conducted by a committee headed by Sen. Hugo Black (now associate justice of the Supreme Court) which exposed undesirable practices in private utility financing and paved the way for Federal legislation regulating public utility holding companies. Similarly, an investigation conducted by Sen. Robert M. La Follette, Jr., of Wisconsin in the thirties which disclosed some of the worst aspects of labor-management relations, led to Federal legislation. The primary purpose of the House Committee on Un-American Activities, which has existed since 1938, is to expose the activities of the Communist Party and of persons alleged to be Communists; it has proposed only one or two minor bills during its history.

Investigations constitute a powerful weapon of Congress; if used wisely and in the public interest they may be as effective as legislation in correcting shortcomings in the administration of the departments or undesirable practices in the economy or society. Congress often uses investigations to expose conditions or practices which warrant public attention and concern, as for example, the investigations of organized crime by the Kefauver committee in the fifties. The celebrated Teapot Dome investigations of the scandals of the Harding administration revealed huge frauds and forced the retirement of several members of the Cabinet from office and led to the conviction of several high officials. The investigations of the Internal Revenue Service during the Truman administration led to its reorganization and reform, as well as the prosecution of several collectors for frauds or misconduct. And the investigation of regulatory commissions during the Eisenhower administration exposed improper political influences and led to the resignation of Sherman Adams, the President's chief adviser and assistant.

Recent Senate investigations of labor racketeering resulted not only in legislation but also in forcing labor organizations to clean house; investigations of some business practices have had a similar effect. Congress has no greater or more important function than that of serving as the "Grand Inquest" of the nation, inquiring not only into the performance of the executive departments, but also into social and economic conditions that need correction.

The importance of legislative investigations was stated by Woodrow Wilson in his classic study, *Congressional Government*:

> Unless Congress have and use every means of acquainting itself with the acts . . . of the administrative agents of the government, the country must be helpless to learn how it is being served; and unless Congress both scrutinize these things and sift them . . . the country must remain . . . in ignorance of the very affairs which it is most important that it should understand.

HISTORY The first congressional investigation, which was conducted in 1792, was concerned with the reasons for the disastrous defeat of General St. Clair and the expedition that he led to put down uprisings by Indian tribes in the Northwest Territory. In 1792 the House of Representatives considered requesting President Washington to make such an inquiry, but in the belief that such a request might be an encroachment on the Executive, decided that since public moneys were voted for the expedition, the House had the right to make an investigation. The select committee which was appointed to conduct the inquiry called upon Secretary of War Knox to supply it with the various papers and documents relating to the expedition. President Washington consulted his Cabinet, which decided that it was within the province of Congress to conduct such inquiries, and that such papers should be submitted "as the public good would permit," but that the President should withhold papers whose disclosure "would endanger the public." Washington instructed the Secretary of War to follow this policy and thus established a rule that has been followed by all Presidents.

The investigation absolved General St. Clair and placed the blame on the War Department and the Treasury for failing to supply the necessary equipment, clothing, and matériel for the mission; but for political reasons the report was never published. The Federalists in Congress feared it would reflect on the Secretaries of War and the Treasury. For 20 years General St. Clair, a broken and impoverished man, pleaded in vain for the publication of the report. Congress refused to pay his claim for out-of-pocket expenses that he had advanced, but shortly before his death voted him a pension of $60 per month. Many years later it repented of its parsimony and voted a substantial sum to his heirs.[1]

Congress made relatively little use of investigations prior to the Civil War. Only 30 investigations were conducted during the first twenty-five years following 1789; most of these concerned matters relating to its own members. All but three were conducted by the House of Representatives.[2] President Jackson and other Presidents at times resisted investigations of the work of executive departments. In 1837 Jackson sent a blistering letter to a House investigating committee that had called on the departments to supply a list of all officers and employees who had been appointed without legal authority, stating its inquiry resembled the Spanish Inquisition. A majority of the committee agreed with him and withdrew the request.

One of the most famous investigations ever conducted by Congress was that by the joint committee set up in 1861 to investigate the con-

[1] See Telford Taylor, *Grand Inquest,* Simon and Shuster, Inc., New York, 1955, chap. 2.
[2] Marshall Dimock, *Congressional Investigating Committees,* The Johns Hopkins Press, Baltimore, 1929, p. 58.

duct of the Civil War. After the Union Army's defeats at Ball's Bluff and Bull Run, the "radical" faction in Congress created the joint committee, whose purpose was not to investigate the causes of lost battles, but to keep informed on military plans and operations and to direct the President in the conduct of the war. Although not a single member of the committee had had military training or experience, it did not hesitate to meddle in military operations, to insist upon being informed about secret war plans, to demand the removal of generals it did not like, and to play favorites in pressing others upon Lincoln. At times Lincoln refused to accept the dictation of the joint committee, but after stormy sessions he sometimes yielded to its wishes. The leading historian of the joint committee appraised its role as a "full-throated attempt on the part of Congress to control the executive's prosecution of the war."[3]

The administration of President Grant witnessed a large number of inquiries into charges of corruption and maladministration, but they produced little result, and the investigating zeal of Congress soon waned. The next spurt of investigations followed the end of World War I, when the Republicans captured control of Congress and instituted 51 investigations of the conduct of the war. After the 1920 election the public grew tired of these investigations and they were brought to an end.

A few years later Congress conducted probably the most notable investigations in its history, exposing the corruption in the Harding administration. These investigations drove from office three members of Harding's Cabinet and other high officials. The frauds disclosed in the leasing of the great Teapot Dome and Elks Hill naval oil reserves were called "the greatest political scandal of this or any other generation." The investigation of the office of the Attorney General and the Veterans Administration brought other serious frauds and official misconduct to light. "Scarcely a corner of the administration escaped inquisition. . . . Upwards of two score inquests were instituted by Congress, through its committees, into the official behavior of the executive branch of the government."[4] Those in charge of the investigations, however, were denounced in the press as "scandalmongers" and "assassins of character"; one writer referred to them as the "sena-

[3] T. Harry Williams, *Lincoln and the Radicals*, University of Wisconsin Press, Madison, Wis., 1941, p. 71.
[4] George B. Galloway, "The Investigative Function of Congress," *American Political Science Review*, 1927, vol. 21, p. 47.

torial debauch of investigations—poking into political garbage cans and dragging the sewers of political intrigue." There can be no doubt, however, that the investigations exposed corruption in government and forced a housecleaning after the executive officers had failed to take any action.

After this wave of congressional investigations ended, the number declined. Up to 1925, according to a careful study, a total of 285 investigations had been conducted.[5] Approximately one hundred of these were conducted in the aftermath of World War I and during 1923–1924. Prior to World War I each Congress had conducted, on the average, no more than two or three investigations, and many of these were very small affairs, involving only one or two days of hearings. Since World War II, however, the number, scope, and cost of investigations have increased enormously. Recent Congresses have undertaken approximately one hundred separate investigations at a cost of some $10 million annually, not including expenditures paid out of regular funds allocated to the standing committees. Thus, the conduct of investigations has become a major activity of Congress.

The tremendous growth of investigations in the last two decades has been due to several factors. During much of this period Congress has been in control of the party or coalition opposed to the President, a situation which always leads to increased investigations. Many investigations are motivated by political considerations and are undertaken at the behest of the opponents of the President, in order to embarrass him and his administration. Until relatively recent years the party leaders of the House of Representatives, if they belonged to the President's party, were able to prevent the authorization of investigations that might harass the administration. For this reason the House conducted few investigations, except when it was in the hands of the party opposed to the President. Formerly it was the Senate, where party control was relatively weak, that conducted most of the investigations of the administration.

In recent years, however, the House has relaxed its controls and today conducts as many investigations as the Senate. Investigations have also increased because Congress has become much more generous in voting funds for its own activities. The government has become vaster in size and complexity and more investigations are required if Congress is to watch over its activities. In addition, a number of members of Congress have risen to national prominence overnight by virtue of their

[5] *Ibid.*

investigative activities. President Truman was nominated for the vice presidency because of the national reputation which he acquired by his skillful conduct of the Senate investigation of industrial mobilization for World War II. Senators Nixon, Kefauver, and McCarthy were brought into the national limelight by their conduct of investigations, a fact that was not lost on their colleagues.

LEGALITY The authority of Congress to conduct investigations incident to legislation has never been questioned. The Supreme Court decided in 1880 in the case of *Kilbourn v. Thompson* (103 U.S. 68), that Congress did not have power to conduct investigations unrelated to legislation. This ruling, however, was modified by later decisions which increased the scope of permissible investigations. In *McGrain v. Daugherty* (273 U.S. 135), the Supreme Court in 1927 upheld the power of a Senate committee to inquire into the private financial affairs of a Cabinet member.

The authority of congressional committees to require witnesses to testify as to their political beliefs and associations, particularly whether they are or formerly were members of the Communist Party, and to disclose the names of other persons whom they believe to have been Communists, has frequently been challenged in the courts. Witnesses may avoid answering such questions by pleading their rights under the Fifth Amendment, which provides that "no person . . . shall be compelled in any criminal case to be a witness against himself." Most persons, however, are reluctant to enter this plea, which is popularly regarded as a confession of guilt. Many witnesses who were willing to testify as to whether they are or formerly were members of the Communist Party have entered the plea of the Fifth Amendment in order to avoid testifying concerning the political beliefs and associations of others.

In the case of *Watkins v. United States* [354 U.S. 178 (1957)], Watkins testified that he had never been a member of the Communist Party but declined to testify as to other individuals, pleading that the House Un-American Activities Committee did not have the right under the First Amendment, which guarantees freedom of speech and assembly, to require him to answer such questions. The Supreme Court sustained his plea, holding that Congress has no general authority to expose the private affairs of individuals without justification in terms of the functions of Congress. The Court held that without specific legislative authorization, a committee cannot legally require a witness to answer questions about his beliefs and associations unless such questions are clearly relevant to the purpose of the inquiry. Two years later, however, the Supreme Court held in the case of *Barenblatt v. U.S.* [360 U.S. 109 (1959)] that a committee inquiring into Communism in education could require Barenblatt, a former assistant at the University of Michigan, to testify whether he had been a member of the Communist Party. A majority of the Court held that the question was relevant to the inquiry.

Another issue which has frequently arisen relates to the power of the President and the departments, acting under his instructions, to withhold confidential papers called for by congressional committees. The right of the President to withhold such information and to instruct the departments not to furnish confidential papers is well established and has been exercised by practically all Presidents since Washington's time.

CRITICISMS AND PROPOSED REFORMS   Many criticisms have been voiced of congressional investigations in recent years, especially because of the excesses of a few committees. At one time during the height of the McCarthy investigations, Walter Lippmann warned that unless congressional investigations were curbed they would bring about a fundamental change in the Constitution. It cannot be doubted that great harm was done to the security of the country by some investigations which professed to safeguard it. The investigation of the Voice of America conducted by the late Senator McCarthy of Wisconsin seriously injured our prestige and relations with other countries at a time when the country was engaged in a bitter struggle with Communism. The investigating activities of the House Un-American Activities Committee have been the subject of serious controversy for years. Thoughtful citizens deplore some of the tactics used by the committee and its violation of the rights of witnesses. Others have defended the committee on the ground that these tactics are necessary to expose the Communist conspiracy. The House of Representatives adopted a code of procedure for its committees in 1955 which is designed to prevent some of the actions which have been most criticized in the past, and several of the Senate committees have adopted similar rules of procedure which are intended to assure witnesses of their rights. But there is no effective way to enforce such rules. Some of the investigations most criticized for violating individual rights have been conducted by committees with admirable rules of procedure.

The major criticisms voiced against congressional investigations include the following: (1) Investigations are often inspired by partisan or factional reasons, and are undertaken not to ascertain the facts and to recommend legislation, but rather to embarrass the party in power. (2) Because of partisanship, they are often conducted in a biased manner and do not win the confidence of Congress and the public. (3) They are expensive, disruptive of administration, and often fail to bring about needed improvements. (4) They are usually inefficient because members of Congress seldom have the expert knowledge or sufficient time to conduct a thorough inquiry. (5) Congress conducts too many investigations, often aimed at securing publicity rather than facts. Many investigations are conducted to advance a particular policy desired by its sponsors. For example, the late Senator McCarran of Nevada conducted an investigation intermittently from 1941 to 1947 the purpose of which was to prevent the Interior Department from raising grazing fees.

One of the major reforms proposed is that Congress make greater use of citizen investigating commissions, whose members may be carefully selected for their qualifications and removed from partisan politics. The British government has long used royal commissions to inquire into many of the great problems of society that require legislative action, and Parliament itself, which, as already mentioned, was called the "Grand Inquest," seldom conducts such inquiries. Congress has not shown any enthusiasm for delegating its investigative powers to other bodies, though it has at times created such investigating commissions, as for example, the two Hoover Commissions, which were joint legislative-executive bodies with citizen representation. In recent decades increasing use has been made of presidential commissions, which correspond to the royal commissions in Great Britain, to conduct inquiries into major public needs and problems.

CONGRESSIONAL CONTROL OF ADMINISTRATION

One of the most important functions of Congress, and one to which it gives the greater part of its time, is to exercise control over the executive departments and agencies.[6] This control, or "oversight" as it is sometimes called, supplements that exercised by the President and the

[6] The following account is based largely on the author's study, *Congressional Control of Administration*, The Brookings Institution, Washington, D.C., 1963. See also John D. Millett, *Government and Public Administration*, McGraw-Hill Book Company, Inc., 1959; and Charles Hyneman, *Bureaucracy in a Democracy*, Harper & Row, Publishers, Incorporated, New York, 1950.

department heads. Some writers have likened Congress to a board of directors whose function is to direct and supervise the operations of a corporation. The analogy is not particularly helpful, for the functions of Congress are quite different from those of a board of directors of a corporation. The supervision of the executive departments is assigned by the Constitution to the President.

Congress has the important functions of creating departments and agencies, authorizing and regulating their activities, watching over their work, checking their performance, and holding them accountable. In performing these functions Congress should take care not to encroach on the functions of the Chief Executive, as a board of directors avoids encroaching on management's functions. There are certain types of control which only the President and the departments can exercise, and other controls which are best exercised by the legislative body.

The purposes of legislative control of administration may be stated broadly as follows:

1. To ascertain whether legislative policies are being faithfully, effectively, and economically carried out, and to hold executive officers accountable for any shortcomings in administration.

2. To determine whether the objectives of legislation are being fully accomplished and to ascertain whether additional legislation is needed.

3. To assure that the laws are being administered in the public interest and to encourage diligence on the part of executive officers in the performance of their duties.

4. To discover any abuses of administrative discretion or improper conduct of executive officers, and to require corrective action.

5. To check internal management controls to see that they are adequate and effective.

6. To hold executive officers accountable for their use of public funds.

The primary concern of the legislature is to secure vigorous, competent, and efficient execution of public policies. The administration of the Federal government was never so important as it is today. The United States cannot meet its new responsibilities of world leadership and cope with the increasingly complex and difficult problems at home unless it is assured of strong, capable administration. For these reasons legislative control of administration must be viewed in the larger perspective of whether it advances or hampers able and efficient administration.

In a democracy legislative control and oversight is essential to see that the policies adopted by the politically responsible officers are being carried out. Excessive control, however, should be avoided, for it deprives executive officers of needed discretion, hampers their initiative, and weakens their accountability. Congress has often imposed highly detailed controls over the operations of the departments, and congressional committees have at times attempted to dictate day-to-day administrative decisions. We live today in the age of the administrative state; it must be democratically controlled but not enfeebled by excessive controls.

Congress exercises control over the executive departments in a number of ways, formal and informal. Formal controls are exercised (1) by enacting statutes which establish and regulate the activities of departments, (2) by voting appropriations,[7] and (3), as we have seen, by conducting investigations of administration. In addition, the Senate exercises control over administration by its power to approve or disapprove the President's nominations to Federal offices.[8] In recent years a new form of congressional control of administration, known as the "legislative veto," has come into use.

LEGISLATIVE CONTROL THROUGH STATUTES   It is through statutes that Congress officially speaks. Statutes create the executive departments and agencies, provide for their principal officers, authorize their activities, and in some instances prescribe their internal organization. About half the bureaus within the executive departments and agencies are provided for by law, and the others have been created by executive action. Executives prefer that Congress leave the creation of bureaus and other internal organizational units to executive discretion, thus permitting internal reorganizations to be made when necessary for improved administration. If bureaus or offices are created by statutes, the effect is to put them on a statutory pedestal, removing them to some extent from overhead direction and supervision, and making it difficult to reassign functions when desirable to promote efficiency. Since 1939 Congress has granted the President authority to reorganize the executive departments, but has required him to submit his reorganization plans to Congress 60 days before they are to become effective, during which period it may set them aside by resolution of one or both houses. Formerly a concurrent resolution of both houses was required, but in recent years either house is authorized to veto his plans.

Executive departments and agencies may perform only those func-

[7] For an account of congressional review of the budget, see John J. Corson and Joseph P. Harris, *Public Administration in Modern Society*, McGraw-Hill Book Company, Inc., New York, 1963, chap. 6.
[8] See Joseph P. Harris, *The Advice and Consent of the Senate*, University of California Press, Berkeley, Calif., 1953.

tions which are authorized by law. Statutes authorizing the work of the departments may be couched either in broad terms, permitting executive officers considerable discretion in determining the specific work programs to be undertaken, or may prescribe in great detail the specific activities to be performed. Broad legislation grants discretion to executive officers and permits flexibility of operations, while detailed legislation enhances congressional control and circumscribes the discretion of executive officers. In either case, programs and activities planned by the departments are passed upon by Congress when it appropriates funds.

There has been a tendency in recent years for Congress to enact detailed statutes regulating the operation of the departments. The annotated statutes regulating the armed services, for example, fill approximately a dozen thick volumes, and most other departments have one or more volumes of statutes prescribing their work. More than fifteen hundred statutes regulate the Civil Service. As various studies of Federal administration have pointed out, unnecessarily detailed statutes governing the work of the departments are harmful to good administration, for they impose rigid and often unsuitable procedures that soon become obsolete. Under such detailed legislation the executive departments are unable to adopt improved methods and keep abreast of rapidly changing technological developments.

In recent years Congress has frequently authorized government programs for only one or two years, thus requiring the department to return for new legislation to continue the program. This procedure makes it difficult for the department to plan programs over a period of years and to recruit a qualified staff, and makes it more amenable to direction and supervision by the congressional committee that passes on its legislation. It puts the department on good behavior, for the legislative committee can end the program by failing to take action to extend it.

THE LEGISLATIVE VETO The precedent of the legislative veto of executive plans and decisions was established in 1939 by the Executive Reorganization Act, which provided that the President's reorganization plans must be submitted to Congress 60 days before going into effect, during which period they could be set aside by concurrent resolution. This device was soon extended into other areas of legislation, and within a few years a veto over certain executive acts was given to standing committees. The House and Senate Armed Services Committees, for example, were given the power to approve or disapprove all real estate transactions of the armed services, which must be reported to them in advance. Presidents Eisenhower and Truman both vetoed statutes giving congressional committees a veto of executive decisions as contrary to the Constitution and to good administration, but in various guises the committee veto has continued. It might appear that a committee check on important decisions of executive officers before they are put into effect is a desirable safeguard against hasty and unwise decisions. Its effect, however, is to divide responsibility and often to inject partisan and parochial influences on executive actions.

INFORMAL CONTROLS   In addition to the formal controls exercised through the official actions of Congress, its standing committees exercise more or less continuous informal or unofficial control over the activities of the executive departments. Often the informal controls are more important than the formal ones. Informal control is exercised by the chairmen and other committee members through oral consultations with the department officers, which occur frequently when Congress is in session, and take the form of inquiries, requests, and sometimes instructions. It is not uncommon for a congressional committee to require department officers to consult with it or with the chairman before taking certain actions. The questions which committee members ask during committee hearings and the points of view that they express carry great weight with department officers, in some cases amounting to virtual instructions as to future department actions. These informal controls, which often take place in private conversations, are not subject to review by either house of Congress and hence are open to abuse. Often they are used to advance private and provincial interests and require the departments to take actions that would not be approved by Congress. Behind the informal control is the sanction of formal control through statutes, appropriations, or investigations, which the departments are anxious to avoid.

THE REORGANIZATION AND REFORM OF CONGRESS

Since the end of World War II there has been widespread demand for the strengthening and reform of Congress. The movement for reform arose largely because of the feeling that too much power had been concentrated in the hands of the President and the executive departments during World War II and the crisis years that preceded it, and that the organization and procedures of Congress should be reformed to enable it to meet its increased responsibilities.[9] Since 1900 the President's powers have greatly increased, largely because the expanded functions of the Federal government required strong executive leadership, and it is questionable whether this trend can be reversed.

In 1945 Congress established a joint committee, headed by Sen. Robert M. La Follette of Wisconsin, to inquire into its organization and operations and to recommend reforms. After conducting extended hearings and making special studies, the joint committee submitted a notable report the following year, which led to the passage of the Legislative Reorganization Act of 1946. Although the recommendations of the joint committee were not fully carried out, the act provided for the most important reorganization of Congress in its history. As a result, Congress has acquired a much larger, better qualified, and better paid staff, and its work has been strengthened in various ways.

The most important single feature of the 1946 Legislative Reorganization Act was the reduction in the number of standing committees in the House of Representatives from 48 to 19, and in the Senate from 33 to 15. It must be said, however, that only minor and inactive committees were abolished. The reduction in the number of standing committees led to a reduction in the number of committee assignments of members of the House and the Senate. Initially, members of the Senate served on only two standing committees, and members of the House on only one, but today most senators are assigned to three or more standing committees and many members of the House are assigned to two or more, and, in addition, serve on numerous subcommittees.

The reduction in the number of standing committees has been more than offset by the growth in the use of standing subcommittees. Each of the major committees of each house today utilizes from five to ten standing subcommittees, as a rule, and these subcommittees function largely as semi-independent bodies with their own staffs. A total of around three hundred subcommittees are used at present, not including many *ad hoc* subcommittees created to consider particular bills. The proliferation of subcommittees has been necessary to enable Congress to perform its greatly increased legislative role.

[9] See Thomas K. Finletter, *Can Representative Government Do the Job?*, Harcourt, Brace & World, Inc., New York, 1945; Robert Heller, *Strengthening the Congress*, National Planning Association, Washington, D.C., 1945; Estes Kefauver and Jack Levine, *A Twentieth Century Congress*, Duell, Sloan & Pearce, Inc., New York, 1947; and James M. Burns, *Congress on Trial: The Politics of Modern Lawmaking*, Harper & Row, Publishers, Incorporated, New York, 1949.

A second feature of the Legislative Reorganization Act of 1946 was to provide each standing committee with a professional staff of four members, in addition to its clerical staff. Larger staffs have since been authorized for a number of the major committees of each house. The committee staffs perform an indispensable service. They assemble and analyze pertinent data and put it in a form which makes it usable by busy committee members; arrange for committee hearings; work with the legislative counsel in drafting bills; write the committee reports; conduct research studies; and perform a wide variety of other tasks for the committee and its chairman. Formerly staff positions were filled by patronage appointees of the chairman, but in recent years the standards have been elevated and most staff members today have professional qualifications. Congressional employees are not under a merit system and have no security of tenure. Nevertheless, many committees have a tradition of retaining their staff employees, regardless of changes in the party in control. Salary scales have been increased to a maximum of around $18,000 annually, and Congress is able to recruit better-qualified personnel.

The Legislative Reference Service of the Library of Congress and the Office of Legislative Counsel of the House and Senate have also been greatly enlarged. Congress today is provided with staff services of a quality that was unknown prior to 1946. This has greatly improved the work of the standing committees and subcommittees, and has removed part of the burden formerly placed on individual members.

A third feature of the 1946 act was to increase the salaries of members of Congress and provide them with greater funds for staff assistance. Members of Congress today receive a salary of $22,500, plus a generous retirement system and allowances for travel, correspondence, and other expenses. Each member of the House is provided with an office suite of two rooms, which will be increased when the third House office building is completed, and senators receive much larger quarters in their two office buildings. Each representative is allowed around $50,000 annually for office hire, which he is free to use as he sees fit. In addition, he receives an allowance of $100 monthly to maintain an office in his district. The staff allowance for a senator is substantially higher, depending upon the population of the state which he represents. Membership in Congress has become for most members a full-time job, and more adequate salaries and staff allowances have made service more attractive to persons of ability. When account is taken of the many expenses of members of Congress, their compensation is fully justified.

Several provisions of the 1946 act failed to accomplish their objectives. One such provision called for a "legislative budget"—a resolution to be adopted early in each session fixing a ceiling on appropriations. This provision proved to be unworkable and was soon abandoned. The Joint Committee recommended home rule for the District of Columbia, which would have freed Congress from having to act as a city council for the capital city, a recommendation that the Senate has repeatedly passed, but which the House Committee on the District of Columbia has blocked. The section of the act regulating lobbying contained so many loopholes that it had little effect. (See Chapter 5 above.)

UNFINISHED BUSINESS   The Legislative Reorganization Act of 1946 did not deal with a number of long-recognized weaknesses of Congress. The great powers enjoyed by the standing committees of Congress, and particularly by their chairmen, have long been the subject of criticism. Woodrow Wilson wrote in 1885 that "I know not how better to describe our form of government in a single phrase than by calling it a government by the chairmen of the standing committees of Congress." The standing committees have often been referred to as "little legislatures." The rule of seniority often elevates members of mediocre attainments, the elders of the assembly who come from safe districts, to highly important positions as chairmen of major committees. A large proportion of the chairmen are of advanced age and cannot give their committees the vigorous and competent leadership that is needed. The tradition that a member of Congress, once he is assigned to a standing committee, is entitled to continue on that committee as long as he remains in Congress, regardless of how he votes on measures, makes the member independent of any effective control by the party which he represents or by the house itself.

Another criticism of Congress frequently heard is the arbitrary power lodged in the Rules Committee of the House to block legislation that it dislikes. It is able to prevent the House from even considering measures on which a majority of its members are ready and eager to vote. The Rules Committee was temporarily shorn of its power in 1949 by the adoption of a rule which permitted chairmen of standing committees to call up bills without its permission, but this provision was dropped two years later.

Many proposals have been made that Congress reform its procedure for passing upon the President's budget. The major criticism is that it passes on the budget piecemeal, enacting nearly a score of appropriation acts at each session, each being considered independently of the others. Moreover, tax measures are considered independently of the other financial measures, and are passed on by another set of committees. As a result, Congress never considers the budget as a whole. Each standing committee of Congress passes upon bills authorizing expenditures. Responsibility is thus hopelessly divided among practically all committees of Congress.

One of the major functions of Congress is to check on the administration of the departments and to hold the executive officers to account for carrying out legislative policies and for economical and efficient administration. Congress has never devised effective ways in which to implement the "legislative oversight" function.

It has been proposed that a question period be instituted in Congress, similar to that used daily in the British House of Commons. This practice requires ministers to answer questions put to them by other members and to accept full responsibility for the policies and actions of their departments. It is doubtful that the same procedure could be used effectively by Congress, under a different constitutional system where department heads are not members of the legislative body, but a similar procedure might be used by congressional committees. Department heads testify before congressional committees, but there is no regular or systematic procedure for questioning them about department policies and administration.

One of the principal criticisms of Congress is the provincialism of its members, who tend to consider legislative problems from the standpoint of their own districts rather than that of the national interest. Members of Congress devote a large amount of their time to interceding with departments on behalf of constituents, and seeking appropriations for their own districts. The tradition in this country that members of Congress must reside in the districts which they represent restricts the choice of voters and deters many able persons from becoming candidates.

The only apparent cure for provincialism, as well as for the irresponsibility which Congress occasionally displays, is to strengthen party leadership and discipline in Congress. Our party and election system, however, does not lend itself readily to strong party leadership and disciplined parties. The national parties are, in fact, loose confederations of state and local party organizations, and have little influence in the selection of candidates for Congress. Stronger national parties and greater party leadership in Congress will develop only as the result of evolutionary growth and change over a period of years. Despite its defects, the present party system has substantial merits, which should not be overlooked in any appraisal of American politics.

Review Questions

1. For what purposes does Congress conduct investigations? How effectively do they serve the purposes? Discuss.

2. What lessons can be learned from the experience of the congressional investigation of the conduct of the Civil War?

3. Discuss the major criticisms and proposed reforms of congressional investigations.

4. What are the functions of Congress in exercising oversight of the executive departments? How effectively does Congress perform this function?

5. What is the legislative veto?

6. Discuss the informal controls over administration exercised by congressional committees?

7. What major changes have been made in the organization and staff of Congress since World War II?

8. Discuss the various proposals that have been advanced to strengthen and reform Congress.

For Further Reading

PRESIDENT

BINKLEY, WILFRED E.: *The President and Congress*, Alfred A. Knopf, Inc., New York, 1946.

———: *The Man in the White House*, The Johns Hopkins Press, Baltimore, 1959.

BROWNLOW, LOUIS: *The President and the Presidency*, Public Administration Service, Chicago, 1949.

CHAMBERLAIN, LAWRENCE H.: *The President, Congress and Legislation*, Columbia University Press, New York, 1946.

CORWIN, EDWARD S.: *The President: Office and Powers*, 4th ed., New York University Press, New York, 1957.

FENNO, RICHARD B.: *The President's Cabinet*, Harvard University Press, Cambridge, Mass., 1959.

HART, JAMES: *The American Presidency in Action*, The Macmillan Company, New York, 1948.

HENRY, LAURIN L.: *Presidential Transitions*, The Brookings Institution, Washington, D.C., 1960.

HERRING, PENDLETON: *Presidential Leadership*, Holt, Rinehart and Winston, Inc., New York, 1940.

HOBBS, EDWARD H.: *Behind the President*, Public Affairs Press, Washington, D.C., 1954.

KOENIG, LEWIS W.: *The Invisible Presidency*, Holt, Rinehart and Winston, Inc., New York, 1960.

LASKI, HAROLD J.: *The American Presidency*, Harper & Row, Publishers, Incorporated, New York, 1940.

MILTON, GEORGE FORT: *The Use of Presidential Power*, Little, Brown and Company, Boston, 1944.

NEUSTADT, RICHARD E.: *Presidential Power*, John Wiley & Sons, Inc., New York, 1960.

ROSSITER, CLINTON L.: *Constitutional Dictatorship*, Princeton University Press, Princeton, N.J., 1948.

———: *The American Presidency*, rev. ed., Harcourt, Brace & World, Inc., New York, 1960.

TOBIN, RICHARD L.: *Decisions of Destiny*, Harcourt, Brace & World, Inc., New York, 1961.

WILSON, WOODROW: *Constitutional Government in the United States*, Columbia University Press, New York, 1961.

CONGRESS

ACHESON, DEAN: *A Citizen Looks at Congress*, Harper & Row, Publishers, Incorporated, New York, 1956.

BAILEY, STEPHEN K.: *Congress Makes a Law*, Columbia University Press, New York, 1950.

BARTH, ALAN: *Government by Investigation*, The Viking Press, Inc., New York, 1955.

BERMAN, DANIEL M.: *A Bill Becomes a Law*, The Macmillan Company, New York, 1962.

BYRNES, JAMES M.: *Congress on Trial*, Harper & Row, Publishers, Incorporated, New York, 1949.

CARROLL, HOLBERT N.: *The House of Representatives and Foreign Affairs*, The University of Pittsburgh Press, Pittsburgh, Pa., 1958.

DAHL, ROBERT A.: *Congress and Foreign Policy*, Harcourt, Brace & World, Inc., New York, 1950.

DRURY, ALAN: *Advise and Consent*, Doubleday & Company, Inc., New York, 1959.

GALLOWAY, GEORGE B.: *The Legislative Process in Congress*, Thomas Y. Crowell Company, New York, 1953.

GRIFFITH, ERNEST S.: *Congress: Its Contemporary Role*, New York University Press, New York, 1951.

GROSS, BERTRAM: *The Legislative Struggle*, McGraw-Hill Book Company, Inc., New York, 1953.

HARRIS, JOSEPH P.: *The Advice and Consent of the Senate*, University of California Press, Berkeley, Calif., 1953.

HAYNES, GEORGE H.: *The Senate of the United States* (2 vols.), Houghton Mifflin Company, Boston, 1938.

HYNEMAN, CHARLES S.: *Bureaucracy in a Democracy*, Harper & Row, Publishers, Inc., New York, 1950.

MATTHEWS, DONALD R.: *U.S. Senators and Their World*, The University of North Carolina Press, Chapel Hill, N.C., 1960.

TAYLOR, TELFORD: *Grand Inquest: The Story of Congressional Investigations*, Simon and Shuster, Inc., New York, 1955.

TRUMAN, DAVID: *The Congressional Party*, John Wiley & Sons, Inc., New York, 1959.

WAHLKE, J. C., and H. EULAU (eds.): *Legislative Behavior: a Reader in Theory and Research*, The Free Press of Glencoe, New York, 1959.

WHITE, WILLIAM S.: *Citadel: The Story of the U.S. Senate*, Harper & Row, Publishers, Inc., New York, 1956.

WILSON, WOODROW: *Congressional Government*, Meridian Books, Inc., New York, 1956.

YOUNG, ROLAND: *The American Congress*, Harper & Row, Publishers, Inc., New York, 1958.

Index

Adams, Sherman, 103
Administration, congressional control of, 109–113
Administrative management, definition, 27
  President's Committee on, 28
Adversary relationship of President and Congress, 56, 62
AFL (see American Federation of Labor)
Altgeld, Governor of Illinois, 39
  (See also Pullman strike of 1894)
American Federation of Labor (AFL), in fair labor standards fight of 1938, 54–56
  in Price Control Act fight of 1946, 45
American Medical Association (AMA), 90
American Political Science Association, proposed reforms of party system, 58
American Railway Union in Pullman strike of 1894, 38–40
Appointment power of President, 22–27
  (See also Removal power)
Appointments, Senate's approval of, 22, 76
Appropriation acts, 117

Bagehot, Walter, 8, 13, 16
Baker v. Carr, 67
  (See also Reapportionment)
Bank of the United States, Jackson's controversy over, 24–27
Bankhead, Senator, 44
Banking and Currency, Committee on, Senate, in price control fight of 1946, 43–46
Barbary pirates, war against, 36
Barenblatt v. United States, 108
Barkley, Alben, 78
Benton, Thomas, 26
Berlin question, 37
Bevan, Ernest, 16
Bicameral legislature, adoption of, 66
Biddle, Nicholas, 25
Bills, kinds of, 83
  numbers before Congress, 82
  origins of, 82–86
Black, Hugo, 102
Bowles, Chester, 46

Budget, Congress' failure to pass on as whole, 116
  legislative, failure of, 116
Budget, Bureau of, clearance of legislative proposals, 84
  Director of, 22
  in Executive Office of President, 29
  functions of, 29
  as major staff assistance to President, 28
Burke, Edmund, 69

Cabinet, as counsel to President, 57
  proposed legislative, 57
Calendars, House, kinds of, 92
  Senate, 95
Calhoun, John, 19
Campaign expenditures of Congressmen, 69
Cannon, "Uncle Joe," Speaker of House, 72
Capehart, Homer, 44
Censure, of Jackson in Bank fight, 25
  expunged, 26
  of Joseph McCarthy, 65
Central Intelligence Agency (CIA), 31
Central Statistical Board, 29
Chiang Kai-shek, 10
China, People's Republic of, intervention in Korea, 10–13
CIO (see Congress of Industrial Organizations)
Civil Service Commission, 28
Clay, Henry, Bank of United States controversy, 24
  on filibuster, 96
  Nullification Ordinance controversy, 19
Cleveland, Grover, in Pullman strike, 38–40
  vetoes, 51
Cloture, 97
Commander in Chief, President as, 12
Committee chairmen, 80
  geographical distribution, 81
  selection by seniority, 80
Committee hearings, 87–89
Committee staff, increase in, 115
  selected by chairman, 80
Committee system, 8

Committee system, assignments under, 79
  changes in 1946, 114
  in Congress, 78–81
Committee of the Whole, 93
Conference committee in Congress, 79
  in fair labor standards fight, 55–56
Confirmation, Senate's power, 76
Congress, as confederation of committees, 7, 116
  control of administration, 109–113
    means, 111–113
      informal controls, 113
      legislative veto, 111–113
      statutes, 111
    purposes, 110
  cooperation with Executive, 56–59
  declaration of war, 37
  discipline of members, 65
  executive reorganization, approval of, 28, 111
  functions and powers, 62–66
    conduct of investigations, 63
    control of administration, 63
    educating and informing public, 64
    other, 64–66
    passing laws, 62
  inability to formulate policy, 7
  investigations, 102–109
    (*See also* Investigations)
  personnel, 71
  proposed reforms, 116–118
  punishment of contempt, 65
  representation, 7
  sources of conflict with President, 43
  staff augmented, Legislative Reference Service, 115
    Office of Legislative Counsel, 115
  treaty making, influence on, 34
  war powers, 35
Congress of Industrial Organizations (CIO), fair labor standards fight of 1938, 54–56
  Price Control Act fight of 1946, 45
Congressional investigations, 102–109
"Congressionalism," 44
Congressmen, role of, 69–71
Consent calendar, 92
Constituencies, local basis of, 7, 117
Constituents, demands on Congressmen, 70
Consulted, President's right to be, 8–13, 27
Contempt of Congress, 65
Cooperation, President and Congress, 56–59
Corwin, Edward S., 26

Council of Economic Advisers, 31
Courtesy of Senate, 77
Czechoslovakia, 16

Debate, 64
  in House, 94
  in Senate, 98
Debs, In re, 39
Declaration of war, 37
Democracy, rise of, 5
Democratic caucus, 74
Democratic committee assignments, 79
Departments and agencies, no reference to, in Constitution, 24
  submission of bills by, 83–85
Discharge petition, procedure for, in House, 92
  in Senate, 95
  use in 1938, 55
District of Columbia, home rule, 116
Duane, William J., 25, 26

Eisenhower, Dwight D., 85, 113
Election of House members, 68–71
Electoral College, 3
Encourage, President's right to, 13–16
European Recovery Act, 15
  (*See also* Marshall Plan)
Executive departments, congressional control over, 109–113
  drafting of bills, 83–85
Executive Office of the President, components of, 30
  formation of, in 1939, 29
  as staff to President, 28
Executive power vested in President, 21
Executive Reorganization Act of 1939, 28, 112
Executive secrecy in investigations, 108
Executive session in considering bills, 88

Fair Labor Standards Act of 1938, 54–56
Federal Reserve Act, 50
Federal troops, use of, by President, 18, 36, 39
The Federalist, 34, 90
Fifth Amendment in congressional invesigations, 107
Filibuster, 95–99
  cloture attempts, 97

Filibuster, history, 96
  use, 95
Finer, Herman, 50
"Fireside chat," Roosevelt's use of, 48
Floor leaders, majority and minority, 75, 77
Folkways of Senate, 76
Foreign policy, President's role in, 31–34
Foreign Relations, Committee on, Senate, 75
Formosa, 10, 85
Friction, proposals to lessen between President and Congress, 56–59

Galloway, George B., 57, 90
Genet affair, 31
Gerry, Elbridge, 67
Gerrymandering, 67
Grant, Ulysses S., 105
Greek-Turkish Aid, Marshall Plan, 13–16

Hamilton, Alexander, on Barbary pirates war, 37
  on neutrality proclamation, 33
Harding, Warren G., 105
Harriman, Averell, 10
Hearings, function of, 85, 87–89
Hind's and Cannon's Precedents of the House of Representatives, 91–92
Hoffman, Paul G., 15
House calendars, 92
House Committee on Un-American Activities (HUAC), 102, 108
House Manual, 91
House of Representatives, calendars, 92
  code for investigations, 108
  committee system, 78–81
  Committee of the Whole, 93
  discharge petition, 92
  Labor Committee, 55
  length of service, 72
  limited debate, 94
  personnel, 71
  procedure in, 91–94
  rules for bills, 93
  Rules Committee, 73, 116
  seating of members, 65
  Speaker and duties, 72
  voting, 93
House and Senate Armed Services Committees, use of legislative veto, 112
HUAC (*see* House Committee on Un-American Activities)

Impeachment, 22, 65
In re Debs, 39
Informal controls over administration, 113
Injunction, use of, in Pullman strike, 39
Interest groups, 89–91
  (*See also* Lobbying)
Internal security, President's responsibility for, 38–40
Investigations by Congress, 102–109
  abuses revealed by, 103, 106
  authorization for, 102
  cost of, 106
  criticisms of, 108
  Fifth Amendment in, 107
  first in U.S. history, 103
  issue of executive secrecy, 108
  Joint Committee to Investigate Conduct of the Civil War, 104
  legality of, 107
  number of, in past, 104–106
    yearly, 102
  power delegated to Hoover Commissions, 109
  procedure and codes, 108
  Supreme Court decisions affecting, 107–108

Jackson, Andrew, Bank of United States fight, 24–27
  Nullification Ordinance controversy, 17–19
  proclamation against nullification, 18
  protest at Senate's censure, 26
  refusal to allow House committee to investigate, 104
Jefferson, Thomas, in Barbary pirates military action, 36
  in Genet affair, 32
  "only-channel" doctrine, 31
  vetoes, 51
Johnson, Louis, 11
Johnson, Lyndon B., 78, 80
Joint Chiefs of Staff in Korean War, 10–12
Joint Committee for Reorganization of Congress, 57, 114, 116
Joint Committees of Congress, 78
Joint executive-legislative council, proposed, 57
Joint resolutions, 83

Kefauver, Estes, 56
Kefauver Committee, 103
Kilbourn v. Thompson, 107
Korea, war in, 10–13

La Follette, Robert M., Jr., 96, 102, 112
La Follette-Monroney Committee, 57, 114, 116
Lawyers, dominance in Congress, 71
Leadership, President's role in, 45–56
Legislation, Presidential leadership in, 49, 54, 83, 86
Legislative budget, 116
Legislative control of administration, 109–113
Legislative Counsel, 115
Legislative program, President's role in, 49, 54, 83, 86
Legislative Reference Division, Bureau of Budget, 84
Legislative Reference Service, Library of Congress, 115
Legislative Reorganization Act of 1946, 57, 63, 78, 91, 102, 114–116
Legislative veto, 111–113
Legislators, attorneys as, 71
roles of, 69–71
Lewis, John L., 56
Liaison Office for Personnel Management, 29
Lincoln, Abraham, 105
Lobbying, 89–91
control of, 91, 116
usefulness of, 89
"Logrolling," 71

MacArthur, General Douglas, removal of, by President Truman, 10–13
McCarran, Pat, 109
McCarthy, Joseph, censured by Senate, 65
role in investigations, 107, 108
McGrain v. Daugherty, 107
McLane, Louis, 25
Madison, James, 22, 31, 90
on neutrality proclamation, 33
vetoes, 51
Marshall, George Catlett, 14
Marshall Plan, 13–16
Messages to Congress, President's, 48–50, 86
Mill, John Stuart, 64
Molotov, Vyascheslav, 16
Monroe, James, 17
Monroe Doctrine, 17
Morris, Gouverneur, 6
Morstein Marx, Fritz, 7
Myers v. United States, 23

National Aeronautics and Space Council, 31

National Association of Manufacturers (NAM), in price control fight, 45
National Resources Planning Board, 29
National Security Council, 31
Neustadt, Richard, 52
Neutrality proclamation, 32
Nomination, of Congressmen, 69
of officers by President, 76
Senate confirmation required, 76
Norris, George, 72, 84
Nullification controversy, 17

Office of Emergency Planning, 31
Office of Government Reports, 29
Office of Legislative Counsel, 115
Office of Price Administration (OPA), fight over extension in 1946, 43–46
Office of Science and Technology, 31
"Only channel" doctrine, 31
Overrepresentation of rural areas, 68

Parliamentarian, 92
Party, President as leader of, 53
Party caucus, 74
Party machinery, in House, 74
in Senate, 77
Party system, 52–54
external to Constitution, 52
proposed reforms of, 58, 117
Philadelphia Convention, 4, 58, 66
Pitt, William, 101
"Pork barrel," 71
Posse comitatus, 18
Presidency, aggrandizement of presidential power, 3–8
as elective kingship, 3
"strong," 6
President, appointment and removal power, 22–27
as chief administrator, 27–31
as Chief Executive, 21–27
as Commander in Chief, 12, 34–38
conflict with Congress, sources of, 43
cooperation with Congress, 56–59
executive power vested in, 21
executive reorganization authority, 28–31
in foreign affairs, 31–34
in internal security, 38–40
in international relations the sole medium, 31
as leader of Congress and nation, 45–56
legislative program, 83, 86